Direct Selling

The rOadmap tO success

I0490072

Sanjeev Prajapati

Saffronberry Publishers

London New Delhi New York

Saffronberry Publishers

New Delhi

www.saffronberry.com

First Published by
Saffronberry Publishers 2023

First edition

Cover art by Riya Chatterjee
Editing by David McLeod
Translation by Ankit Singh & team

This book was professionally typeset on Reedsy.
Find out more at reedsy.com

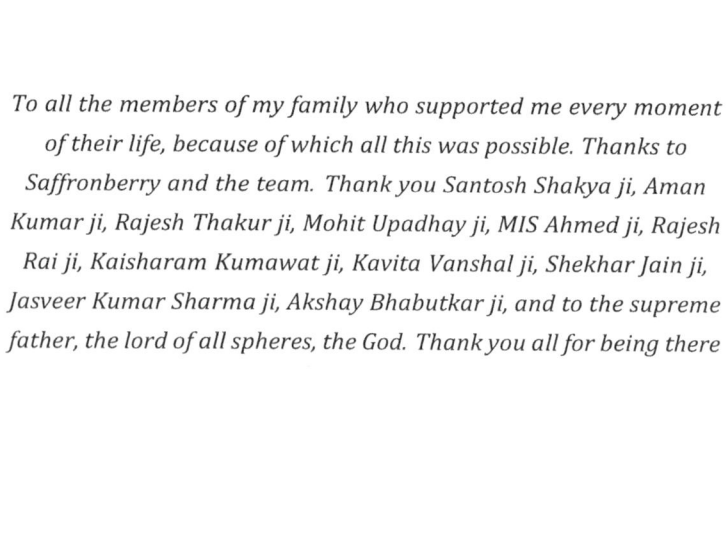

To all the members of my family who supported me every moment of their life, because of which all this was possible. Thanks to Saffronberry and the team. Thank you Santosh Shakya ji, Aman Kumar ji, Rajesh Thakur ji, Mohit Upadhay ji, MIS Ahmed ji, Rajesh Rai ji, Kaisharam Kumawat ji, Kavita Vanshal ji, Shekhar Jain ji, Jasveer Kumar Sharma ji, Akshay Bhabutkar ji, and to the supreme father, the lord of all spheres, the God. Thank you all for being there

"The best marketing doesn't feel like marketing."

Tom Fishburne

Contents

Foreword

So yet again a new book on Network Marketing ? Again a new book talking about the ins and outs of network marketing? Talking about network marketing again? Man, there are surely and most certainly several thousands of books available in the market on the topics, types and methods of network marketing, then who needs this book? I have been in network marketing for about eight years. And during these eight years, every year I used to participate in hundreds of functions, discuss network marketing with thousands of people etc. But for the last few months when I met them (the people) in the network of people of Shikhar, a voice came from the inside of my heart. Which inspired me to write this book. My mind does not want people to struggle their whole life in some business while I am well aware of the tricks of that damn business. There are thousands of books available in the market on network marketing but all those are just plain theories. Very few compilations of practical experiences are available. Therefore, inspired by this inner voice, I began meeting people at the pinnacle of network marketing and invited them to share their experiences in this book. And I was surprised to find that as much as I was elated to share their experiences through a book, I found the same enthusiasm in all of them. They also wanted that whatever they have learned till date in this network marketing business can be taught to the youth of the new generation so that they don't just keep on struggling in this era of modernity. With the inspiration of the soul and with the help of my dear respected colleagues, this book is now available in the market for the youth. I wish this will help the youth in their businesses in every way and they will be able to look at network marketing from a different angle considering it as a business.

-Sanjeev Prajapati.

Preface

Dear Readers... This book brings together the views of experienced players of network marketing for you. Here you will be able to get information on various topics of network marketing at one go. All the authors writing chapters in this have 8 to 10 years of direct selling experience. It is clear from this that this book will prove to be a milestone for the students of direct selling. Keep your mind open while reading this book. Everyone has their own experiences of direct selling and everyone has their own way of presenting it, so while reading the book read the entire book. Many times we do such a thing that we leave the book after reading it half, due to which we do not get any benefit. I request the readers that when you start reading the book, take the time to read it completely. The essence of this book is the network. So this book is dedicated to every network marketing leader who wants to save time and money. The network is such an amazing tool through which every big task seems small and through which we make our dreams fly high. And we get progress in becoming a diamond through our network. The biggest advantage of this book is that all the predefined set of chapters here given in this have been written by people who are doing network marketing themselves and have achieved success. Only the one who has become successful by doing any work can be the best teacher of that subject, that's why this book becomes even more special. This book will tell you the foundation stone of direct selling, direct strategies etc. Stone of prospects, after reading this book you will be able to understand the foundation direct selling, direct selling strategies and possibilities of direct selling. Before starting any business, it is very important to have basic knowledge about it. This book will provide you with the fundamental information about direct selling. The changes that have taken place till date with time, whether it has gone ahead from the agricultural era to today's information age, every small incident of today's time goes viral through social media. This is how direct selling has started a viral era. As I said before, read the book with an open mind and do not get emotional. After reading the book, a sea of thoughts will start flowing in your mind. After reading the book you will see the limitless possibilities of this business. Many questions will arise in your mind after reading the book. If you would like to discuss it with someone or the other, then I would like to give you a suggestion, and here too is one of my suggestion.

D² - Discuss & Decide.

Definitely after reading the book you have to discuss i.e. discuss. One thing to be kept in mind is that you have to do the discussion i.e. discussion only with those who are already doing direct selling and have been successful in doing it. After reading the book and discussing it, you should give the final answer. To take action means you have to decide, means you have to take decision. After that, whatever your decision is, you have to move forward. I am sure that after knowing about the opportunity like direct selling, your decision will be to jump all the way in it. All you have to do is learn direct selling and keep moving forward. Right now I would like to tell you that you should immediately start reading the book. Every thing has a network.

— Sanjeev Prajapati

Sanjeev Prajapati - What you need to know about this viral era of direct selling

How to understand viral marketing

The way corona virus, Ebola virus, or any specific virus fair spreads by virus, within the same way, the promoting of a arrange promoting company can be done as viral promoting. This is often the trick to create your authority viral and your organize, continuously keep in mind that you simply are a magnet, anything comes inside 3 feet sweep of you must come some place in your fork or penetrate.Because networking is an art and it is seriously no joke. Many leaders have learned this art and put it to good use. On an average it comes late in people's understanding. Or else it does not come at all. Those who are understanding this viral era of direct selling, they are working like network making machines, they know that if we do not make someone a part of the network, tomorrow someone else will make it a part of their network. I remember very well when I came to know about the world's beautiful business which is direct selling in 2012, then very few people were familiar with my business but in today's time most of the people are interested in direct. Where is the company? One day, sitting in solitude, contacted the people of my circle through phone calls and did only one thing to them.

Why did you choose network marketing

Everyone said with their optimistic attitude!
1) Making new friend everyday
2) New home
3) Extra income
4) Own business
5) Foreign Trip
6) Jewellery for yourself and your family
7) Extra free time
8) Let people's money work for us
9) Let people's time work for us
10) Let people's skills work for us
11) To make parents go on pilgrimages
12) Personal Development
13) New dream car
14) Retirement with black hair
15) Helping people

Now my two questions with you

1) Why did you choose network marketing?

2) The direct selling in which people have such a positive and optimistic view inside, should such direct selling become the starting point of a viral era or not?

According to me first in direct selling (Network Marketing) you have any one of above given your first priority. Due to which you are in network marketing business. Everyone has a strong reason of his own. Everyone has their own preferences when it comes to network marketing.

If you have a solid reason for any one of your preferences given above, then you will also get all the above mentioned options as a bonus.

Because 1st Direct selling is the only road that is made of the road of your dreams but easily accessible. And it is certainly made up of of these 5 pillars.

Time

Health

Security

Wealth

Respect

A) Time

Nature has not discriminated against your most important possession, time. Everyone has the same amount of time as you. There isn't a single minute that is either more or less. You get 24 hours in your daily quota every day when you wake up, and the most surprising thing is that we get it every day, you eat it every day, no one points a finger at you, even if you spend all of your time, there is no legal action against you, destroy it as you want, you can destroy your present but not even for one futile second of your future, you cannot demand this from God, you cannot demand this from any goddess.

You cannot borrow from anyone, even after all this, we meet again the next day after 24 hours as soon as you wake up in the morning. Your every small or big happiness, money, health and satisfaction, you can make good use of your time in the form of correct time management,

"Don't start your day until you plan to end it" Jim Rohn

Network Marketing is the most efficient method to spend your time. Network Marketing is a family business, and we are the sole proprietors. We plan our own business, including how many days we work in a week and how much work we have to perform in a month. And we decide how many hours we have to work in a day. As a result, the significance of this firm grows with our family. All of the leads that have had remarkable success in direct selling had only 24 hours on average.

You can work only for maximum 12 to 15 hours, but today you have decided to join any direct selling company, if you plan to work, then when will you start working for thousands of hours, because when we have thousands People will become a team, we will not even know. One can never work 1000 hours in a single day but it is much easier through a network this is called time fraternity and strategy.

"If you take your work, awareness and responsibility in the right direction, you will become adept at managing yourself in terms of time" Machen MacDonald.

B) Health

Health is such an art if you learn once then your life will be happy forever

Before making a presentation in front of another person, we make a presentation to ourselves. Running like a job changes our entire eating and drinking regimen, and we lose health as a result. We are all set to live our life profiles in our own unique style in network marketing. We will pay greater attention to ourselves and what we obtain when we have plenty of free time. Coming to a direct selling organization caused me to shift; network marketing is the only source of all-around development in our planet.

C) Security

When we begin any work, a lot of thoughts run through our heads. By working hard in our youth, we may satisfy our need in every way. However, when it comes to old age, people are obliged to believe that this is the reason why individuals seek government jobs. Once you've established your network in network marketing, knowledge is passed down from generation to generation according to the rules of any direct selling firm. If for any reason the network created by you and in the meantime, if any accident happens, then the entire network is transferred to the name of your nominee, you do not need to start from scratch. I meet many such families who are still achievers even after a decade in their families. That's why network marketing provides security to you and your family. That's why network marketing is a business of immense potential.

D) Wealth

"If you are born in a poor family then it is not your fault but if you die in a poor family then it is your fault" - Bill Gates

Every person has a chance to succeed, and one such opportunity is presented through Network Marketing. By putting in some effort today, you can achieve significant results in a couple of years. Although initially, your hard work may yield less output, after a year or two, you will have to put in less effort. I once heard a story from a friend about the Chinese Bamboo, and it made me feel inspired. It made me realize that the Chinese Bamboo teaches us about the importance of patience in achieving success. We need to be patient and have faith in our abilities to influence development and bring about positive change.

Story of Chinese Bamboo

Like every tree plant, Chinese bamboo also needs nutrients for its growth. Fertilizers, water, air and fertile soil, in this way we do this work continuously for 1 year, taking care of it in every way, the way we take care of our team in dry days, we do it for 1 year, but feeling it dry in 1 year and then when we do not see any difference in any kind of activity nor do we see any symptoms in that Chinese bamboo. In the same way in the second year, also the same fertilizers, water and timely care, but in the second year also there is no tree of any kind. It also works in the same way. We think that it is very difficult (fertilizer water care) but there is no idea of the results. It is the test of our patience and dedication, and in no time, the Chinese experience a wonderful development in the fifth year. The vine grows 70 to 90 feet in six to eight weeks (about 2 months) after flowering. Seeing all this, we do not believe, because we have seen about 4 years of the beginning, such a network is made after many years of beginning, descending on the ground level. You put in strengthening the underground root like that Chinese bamboo. If you don't make yourself strong like a Chinese bamboo, then how will you make such a huge body of 70 to 80 feet, so be patient towards your meaningful dreams and goals and face adverse circumstances. All this is due to our success. You keep working with patience, you will never know when you will cross six figure income, because here we do not work alone, we have thousands of hands and thousands of brains working here. That's why our network is our real asset. You just work on building a network, wealth will be created automatically.

E) Respect

The network marketing business model is rapidly gaining popularity in our country. This model not only helps us achieve success but also contributes to our personal development. In contrast to the traditional approach of gaining popularity through expensive political campaigns, in network marketing, your team members can effortlessly sell out all the tickets for your grand sale or tax seminar through word of mouth.And when there is a celebration, your team members shower you with flower garlands and this celebration is no less than a wedding celebration, this type of celebration happens every month and two-three times a year, whatever and wherever you are in. No one else knows the environment and atmosphere there more than you. As soon as you retire from your profession and you get a chance sometime in the future, then you will feel that it is worth it to become a direct selling business. Money is the top thing for everyone, which is available in the form of direct selling business. In this way the five pillars of direct selling are:

1) Time

2) Health

3) Security

4) Wealth

5) Fame

All these are done through network marketing so direct selling is the beginning of a viral era and be in the place of this beginning. You and your family will always feel happy.

2

Santosh Shakya - Business with great potentials

Direct selling is a business that I consider to be full of endless possibilities. Although it's not possible to cover the entirety of direct selling in one article due to its vastness, I will attempt to showcase its limitless potential through this brief article.

Currently, direct selling is a crucial topic for global business leaders. Even Bill Gates, the founder of Microsoft, was once asked what he would do if he lost all his business, to which he famously replied that he would start anew with network marketing.

Nowadays, prominent business figures, such as former US President Donald Trump and the world's largest business coach Robert Kiyosaki, among others, are promoting network marketing as a viable business option.

Selling: The Road to Riches

I recently read "The Number One Salesman in the World" by Joe Girard, a renowned global salesman. In his book, Girard emphasizes that selling is the only profession where one can aspire to achieve wealth and actually become rich. In any business, sales are the primary source of revenue; everything else is just an expense. Therefore, the individuals who sell the products or services are the most critical component of the organization, as they are responsible for generating income. Without good salespeople, a company cannot achieve significant growth.

The act of selling goods is the most crucial job in the world. If you possess the ability to sell, you have the potential to become the wealthiest person on the planet. On the other hand, if you lack sales skills, someone else will take advantage of your talent to become rich themselves. In any business organization, salespeople are the only individuals who have the opportunity to earn unlimited incentives. The more you sell, the higher your incentives will be.

Direct Selling: The Greatest Opportunity

The world's most successful business leaders are endorsing direct selling or network marketing. This indicates that it is a remarkable opportunity, as it is rare for the world's top companies to offer such a chance to customers. With direct selling, customers have the right to sell the products themselves. Even if they don't make a sale, they can still profit simply by introducing new customers to the product. The company offers incentives for doing so. Some might argue that commission is also given to shopkeepers who sell the product, so what makes direct selling so special? The reason I call direct selling the greatest opportunity in the world is because of its unique qualities and benefits.

1. In contrast to traditional retail where the shopkeeper has to invest a significant amount of money to become a retailer for a company, direct selling requires no investment at all. You can join the company for free and start promoting the products to potential customers. Unlike traditional businesses, where only wealthy individuals can afford to invest and start a business, direct selling offers everyone an equal opportunity to start a business without any investment. Additionally, direct selling companies provide commission to their salespeople, which is not common in traditional businesses. These unique qualities of direct selling make it an excellent opportunity for those seeking to start their own business.

(A) In a traditional business, you can only become a retailer of the company and cannot recruit others to become retailers, nor can you earn any income from making others a retailer. In contrast, in direct selling, you become a distributor of the company and have the chance to recruit new distributors. You earn income solely from the new distributors you recruit. Some may argue that the company also gives commission to the shopkeeper in traditional business, but this does not compare to the opportunities presented in direct selling. That's why I believe direct selling is the greatest opportunity in the world.

(B) Besides the chance to sell products, direct selling also allows you to earn return on investment (ROI) from the distributors you recruit. ROI is considered the most self-sufficient income in the world as you put in the effort once and get a lifetime income in return.

2) Traditional businesses require you to establish your own shop and have a large warehouse to store the products, but in direct selling, there is no need to maintain a warehouse because the company takes care of it. The products are stored in the company's warehouse and you can take them as per your requirement.

3) In traditional business which also run in the form of franchise, you have to pay crores of rupees as security but in direct selling the company cannot take any kind of security.

4) There are many companies which give you opportunity to do business all over the world.

5) In traditional business, when you invest Crores of rupees, you have to face the risk of losing your business, but in direct selling business, you do not make any investment, when you do not make any investment, then there is no risk of losing your business, that simple does not happen. Ever.

6) One more thing that makes direct selling special is that, direct selling gives you an opportunity to build a business according to

your ability. There is no limit in this, you can make the business as big as you want and earn money according to your wishful work.

7) The products being sold through direct selling are of good quality as one only encourages these products to be used by one's own personal relatives, one who will not use the product himself, can't be always motivated to tell about that product. For sure.

8) Direct selling is unique in that it can be pursued as a part-time endeavor in addition to one's job or other business. This is a significant advantage for individuals who rely on their current employment to support their families. Many people in this situation harbor a desire to pursue entrepreneurship, and direct selling offers an opportunity to do so without having to quit their job.

"Direct selling is a new way of doing business and a unique way to earn money." - Santosh Shakya

Direct Selling: Personal Training & Vocational Education

Direct selling teaches ordinary people the essential aspects of business that lead to wealth creation. It is a common belief that only those who have a lot of money can become rich, but this is not true. The reality is that anyone can become rich if they have the right business direction, regardless of their background. Direct selling provides that direction and thus offers immense possibilities for success. Direct selling companies teach you everything you need to know about the business, such as how to present the products to potential customers, without requiring you to spend any money or take any courses. This is the greatest advantage of direct selling, as successful leaders of such companies give you the guidance that would cost you thousands of rupees at other institutions. While direct selling can generate income, its greatest benefit is that it empowers people to become successful entrepreneurs. Here's how:

1) Communication skills- When you do business in direct selling business, you get to know how to interact with people.

2) Personal Development- Those courses of personality development which you had to buy in lakhs of rupees, you get that course of personality development through your environment.

3) Public Speaking- People who struggle to communicate in social settings find themselves speaking in front of large audiences in direct selling. Public speaking, which is commonly feared, becomes effortless for them. Direct selling companies provide training in speaking skills and being in that environment automatically helps you develop your speaking abilities.

4) Corporate Culture- The biggest thing is that direct selling companies give you such an environment where your growth starts happening automatically and in a couple of years you find that you have completely changed.

5) Tech Development- Your technical knowledge increases after coming to direct selling because by coming here you can start your business online. You also get guidance on how to do it, how to use technical tools for your development, all these things are taught to you in the name of direct selling company.

Direct selling - The Road to Freedom

Toiling in various professions like jobs, businesses, or small-scale industries, we tend to be absorbed in work 24/7. This often leaves us with no time to spend with our families or even take care of ourselves. In fact, some people are so busy with their work that they fail to notice their children growing up. Due to hectic schedules, people's lives resemble a race track. Despite the availability of freedom, many are trapped and unable to break free. However, direct selling provides an opportunity to escape this dilemma. With direct selling, you can dedicate time to your loved ones and yourself. This business can be started part-time and eventually lead to liberation from the clutches of a busy life.

Money: The first step to freedom

The root cause of your worries is linked to money. If you don't have sufficient funds to meet your and your family's needs, you'll keep striving for money throughout your life. A job provides you with enough money to cover your expenses, but you never gain financial independence. Big businessmen, on the other hand, continue to earn money even if they don't work for several months because their earnings aren't directly linked to their work. Direct selling provides a comparable opportunity. When your team grows, you'll have more free time, and eventually, you'll become entirely free. You'll have plenty of leisure time that you can spend with your family and travel to new places. You'll be able to travel wherever you choose. If you work hard and achieve a high rank in direct selling, you can take long vacations and go on big tours. The liberty I'm referring to is the kind that only successful businessmen can imagine. Direct selling provides the same opportunities as big business, where you'll continue to earn money even if you don't work for a month, two, or three, because your team will continue to work, and you'll earn passive income. At some point, your role will be reduced to training your team.

Direct selling provides you with the opportunity to work at your own pace and choose your own working hours, which is something that everyone dreams of. There are no bosses in direct selling, which means that nobody can tell you how to work or when to work.

As your team grows, you will have more free time to spend with your family and travel to new places. You can go wherever you want and take long vacations if you work hard and achieve a high position in the direct selling industry. This level of freedom is something that only big businessmen can enjoy, but direct selling gives you the same opportunities.

Nirvana- The spiritual form of freedom

Nirvana is the state of being free from all worldly attachments such as ego, greed, and time. It is the ultimate goal of life, and it can only be achieved when you have enough money and time. Direct selling provides an opportunity to fulfill your financial needs and have free time to practice knowledge and attain success on the path to Nirvana. Achieving financial freedom and time independence are essential steps towards attaining the great heights of philosophy. So, if you dedicate yourself to direct selling, you can fulfill your needs and ultimately achieve the ultimate goal of Nirvana.

Shakyamuni Bhagwan Gautam Buddha had said-

"You become what you think"

Think about freedom, make freedom your goal, direct selling is a great opportunity, tap its possibilities and get all the possibilities of life.

3

Rajesh Roy - With network, is the net worth

If you observe the past five to ten years, you will notice a significant rise in the number of self-made millionaires and billionaires. Individuals like Baba Ramdev of Patanjali, Mark Zuckerberg of Facebook, Jeff Bezos of Amazon, Byju Raveendran of Byju's, Bhavish Aggarwal of Ola, Ritesh Agarwwal of Oyo, and Deepinder Goyal of Zomato have all achieved immense success in a short period of time. But how did they achieve it? What is the secret to their success? The common thread among all of them is their adoption of new methods and thinking patterns, departing from traditional ways and embracing new ones. They utilized people as their most valuable resource and were able to achieve greatness by doing so. These individuals started off poor and from humble backgrounds, but they possessed a unique way of thinking and working. They were driven by the passion to pursue their dreams and turn them into reality, and despite facing numerous obstacles, they remained steadfast in achieving their goals. Their net worth today is beyond imagination and a testament to their relentless focus on building their networks with their time, energy, and finances. The key to their success lies in their network-building skills, and if you want to achieve similar success, you must learn to do the same.

The easiest way to network is to connect with people. Connecting with people

It's not uncommon for thousands of people to be connected on my public WhatsApp, but this isn't anything special, as it's a natural part of being human. From the moment we're born, we begin to form relationships with family, friends, and acquaintances that continue throughout our lives. While I personally have relationships with four to five hundred people and many people know me, my net worth isn't increasing. This is because I'm not considering these people as resources, which is likely the missing piece to increasing my net worth.

Shiv Khera ji says – The winner does not do any new work but he does every work in a different way.

He also made people his resource. You didn't consider your acquaintances as resources, but they. You tell me that making likes to people is a wrong thing? Is it wrong to join, help them, move forward?

No ? That means building a network is also not wrong.

But why do people say wrong to the network? One reason for this is that the mood of the people is like this. People in their own families also do not respect brothers and sisters.

May be - they may ask for something sometime, may be they will come from my success.

If you also have such a situation, then I would like to tell you that just look at its other aspect as well.

If you have a strong and positive connection with someone, it may be the case that they will be there for you when you need their help. Especially during challenging times, those individuals whom you trust the most may be the ones who step forward to assist you. It's important to keep in mind that when dealing with issues involving banks, hotels, or any governmental bureaucracy, we often seek out familiar faces in the hopes that they can facilitate our needs. Similarly, when hosting a celebration such as a wedding or party, we tend to reach out first to those whom we have positive relationships with.

Right?

There are two types of people in the world, poor or rich.

Today the rich are getting richer and the condition of the poor remains the same. The rich prepares to build more and more networks so that his net worth increases every year. While the poor is engaged in breaking everything. The rich talk about adding, due to which their net worth increases and the people with poor mentality talk about breaking, due to which they become poorer.

Talking about Ambani, how did he become the richest person in Asia?

Because of the network, everyone now has a Jio sim, which means we are part of their network whether we realize it or not. Even if we don't intend to, we are indirectly contributing to the benefits of the network. You can imagine how much profit Ambani is making from Jio every month. Jio has approximately 80 million customers currently. If each customer generates a profit of 100 rupees per month, then the total monthly income would be 800 crores. This will continue to increase as long as people use Jio.

Ambani achieved that he created a network of eight crore people. Due to which his net worth is increasing by eight hundred crores every month.

You are somewhere in someone's network and someone and the other somewhere is taking advantage, even if it is not an economic advantage.

It means to say that if you also want to get economic benefits, then you will have to increase the network.

Today everyone is taking advantage of the network.

Be it the sea seller, the betle seller, the tea seller, the cloth seller, the milk seller, the knowledge seller, the milk seller, the fast food seller or any other shopkeeper, be it the mall seller or the cart seller?

You tell me at what stage their income would have increased? I know that your answer will be that when maximum number of consumers or customers are with them.

In coaching, in college, when there will be more and more students, when more and more people will come to drink tea at the tea shop.

That is, somewhere the same thing comes on the network. That means every network is using it but using different terminologies, that means it calls it by different names. For example – student for teacher, client for lawyer, professional for door service, customer for shopkeeper etc.

Those who have more people, their income will be more.

But still some people will not accept that they are networking or is the network correct?

The way you put some part of your income here for the future with the thought that you will get more returns. In the same way you also spend some of your time in preparing the network. In just three-four years, you will get such a return, which cannot be found even in a year's job. You will get Time Freedom, Money Freedom.

Possibility of Network in India – The concept of network was first introduced in 1886 when companies realized that the cost of a product increased significantly by the time it reached the end consumer. They realized that if they could directly deliver the goods to the customer, it would not only benefit the customer but also save costs for the company. This would allow the customer to purchase more goods and the company to benefit from increased sales. This concept of buying and selling through direct delivery became the foundation of the network industry, which has now grown into a large industry with many successful individuals living happy lives.

In India also it started in the decade of NE and today in India also Lakhs of people are making their dreams come true through this.

In 2016, a guideline has also been made by the Government of India. People are accepting it now. Doesn't want to do it yet it does. One of the strengths of the network is that no one can create network lines with their own mind. Because the one who had shown knowledge to him, said no to the one he could or could not say no.

I want to convey that whenever there is a new innovation in the world, people tend to resist it. For instance, people had severe objections when computers were introduced, as they feared it would render many people jobless. However, today, can we imagine doing any work without computers? Even if we consider rural areas, we can see that there are four to five shops in the square and intersection, indicating that computers have become an essential part of our lives.

The introduction of online marketing caused panic among

shopkeepers, who feared that their businesses might suffer. However, online marketing has many benefits, such as allowing customers to purchase goods easily without spending hours shopping, saving their time. Many companies in India now use online marketing. However, there are also some disadvantages, such as potential delivery issues and the possibility of receiving a different or fake item. Despite this, people can now buy everything they need online.

When direct selling emerged, there was a lot of opposition and negative opinions about it. People had misconceptions and believed it to be a scheme to trap and fool others. Some companies also used false information to lure people in, resulting in many losing their investments and belongings. This caused a shift in people's mindset, leading to a negative view of direct selling. Some who had invested in these companies had to face the consequences and were left with nothing. Despite the potential of some individuals who were working with faith, many were unsuccessful due to choosing the wrong company, being greedy, or being deceived by seniors, resulting in social isolation. The saying "once bitten, twice shy" holds true for those who were affected by direct selling schemes.

The thing to note is that –
   This is it, sir, it keeps changing.
   Everything passes.
   It is always light after darkness.
   After the festival of sorrows.
   It is always gifts of happiness.
   No matter how expensive the watches are

This is it, sir, it keeps changing.

The black day in the history of Network Indies is about to end. And with a new thinking a new dawn is rising in the second decade of the 20th century. This network is all set to make its mark as the forlorn gone time for Indies.

It is a positive development that companies must operate within the regulations set by the government. Nowadays, companies that have a credible background and produce their own goods are entering the market. The government is currently facing a growing issue of unemployment and black marketing, and they are struggling to combat it. As a result, the government acknowledges the importance of direct selling.

Today two issues are in front of everyone – unemployment and adulterated goods.

If you buy any item, it is for the sake of its quality, but some people also mix it in food items to satisfy the need. And unknowingly, they adulterate things, due to which the common people suffer a lot. But by way of direct selling, you get quality food, that too with pay bills.

Become smart citizens. That means you pay tax to the government on the purchase of every product.

How to do that?

You tell me how many products you use when you wake up in the morning and when you go to sleep at night. You and your family members have been shopping from the shop next to you for 5-10-20 years or your father has also been shopping from the shop he knows all his life.

Tell me what benefit did both of you get? You will say that we got our credit even if we don't have money. Shopkeeper will give us non-essential goods. right there isn't it?

Was anyone able to make a career? Everyone makes a deed, but what about career?

Till now you must have asked 20-50-100 customers to buy goods from that shop. Did that shopkeeper give you any shares? No ?

Would you say that you are crazy? Will that shopkeeper give me shares? The capital is his, the goods are his, he works for many hours in the shop, he bears the profit and loss, so in what happiness will he give me a share ?

I want to tell you both that you have provided the greatest assistance to that shopkeeper by bringing in customers. This means that you have significantly contributed to the expansion of the shopkeeper's network and wealth. Today, you can take pride in the fact that you have been purchasing goods from the same shop for the past 10-20 years. Thanks to your patronage, the shopkeeper now lives in a multi-story house, owns a car, sends his sons to the best colleges, and buys land worth Rs 5-10 lakh every year. This should bring a sense of satisfaction to you, don't you think?

By joining direct selling business, if you try to increase the customer then you had helped, maybe you will make yourself a nice career as well. I want to tell you that the more that today's time is network network one has, the more his net worth keeps increasing.

Net worth – the value of all movable and immovable assets held by you. That is, the value of your land, house, car, shares or everything that you have is called net worth.

As you may have observed, spiders build their webs, creating a network to catch their prey. Through their hard work, they can secure a steady source of food without having to constantly hunt. Similarly, network marketing offers an opportunity to create a network that can lead to a wonderful and prosperous life. Unfortunately, not many people understand the power of this industry, despite the potential it offers.

Your whole life gets set here, yes it gets set.

You must be thinking that if someone gets a government job then his Life also gets set. If you are thinking like this, then read further.

I have a question, do you get security and peace in whatever work you do? And if you get then till when?

Even if God doesn't want the job you are doing, even if something happens to you or you leave this world, then how much benefit will you get in that job? What will be your answer whether you will get benefit? His family will get 50% pension, isn't it?

Let me tell you who are taking pensions today or in the future

Pension = Tension

Pension is always half of the salary. Hey brother, when I was getting full salary, at that time also I was able to survive somehow, now I am getting half salary, what will happen to him?

Nothing will happen that's why I say

that Pension = Tension

But the network itself will be the most emerging business of the coming times. Where anyone can belong to any age, religion, caste, religion, gender and can make his life and the life of his loved ones wonderful.

Your income and reputation in the network keeps on increasing with time.

You have heard that the older the honey, the more effective it will be. Similarly, the older you are in the network, the more your happiness will increase.

You must have heard a quote:

Along with life, even after life.

It is made for 100% network only.

Know one thing, unless there is a purpose, a person does nothing, nothing.

There should be some purpose for doing every work, only then you will be able to do it otherwise not.

I keep telling you below why to network. After checking, which reason would be suitable for you to increase your network and network?

1. If you want to take some additional income along with your income, then do it. You all know that sometimes an event comes without any invitation, due to which people's budget gets spoiled, in that case everyone wishes that maybe if there was some extra income, they could have managed. It is the nature of people to take food – whether it is a good one or a fruitful one. You must have taken some taste from them.
2. If you like to meet new people, then this is the best platform where you will get the opportunity to meet people from all walks of life and make a lot of new friends.
3. If you always want to learn or teach something new, then this will help you to fulfill your desire. This is one such business where your personality takes four months. This ocean can be where you will get a chance to see the beautiful cities of the world, that too off the coast.
4. If you are fond of traveling abroad, then this is the best place for you.
5. Here you can become your own best version.

6. Who doesn't want to earn money? But what if it is about millions? Those who come out of IIT, IIM, only those people get the package of lakhs, but here every person, whether educated or illiterate, male or female, old or tongue-tied, people of every section are earning lakhs, you can also earn.

7. If we talk about respect, then you get more respect, respect and blessings of people than the MLA and MP of your city.

8. If you are worried about the safety of your family, what will happen to your family? Here, after working hard for two to three years, you and your family becomes financially secure.

9. It is a platform that has made many ordinary people special. That is, the network gave a chance to shine. It is the wonder of the network that thousands of people have become motivational speakers, writers, millionaires and businessmen.

10. Network India tells you the importance of time, how valuable your time is. By measuring the time, you can measure your income.

11. This is the only platform where every small and big dream of yours can be fulfilled because here you are not alone, there is an army of thousands of people with you who work for their dreams, their dreams do come true. Yes, your dream also comes true. The dream of many in one comes true here. If one succeeds, then many family members become proud and their faces light up.

12. If anywhere in the world, you will find people who are happy, peaceful, blissful, positive thinking, working for the welfare of society and country, making others successful and having love for all people here. You will find people

who think big, fulfill their dreams and face every challenge firmly.

13. If you aspire to be a job provider rather than a job searcher.

There are two reasons, it is just necessary to look inside yourself, to recognize your own strength – what can you achieve? Do you have the desire to receive? -

God created humans so that they can help each other.

Premchand ji says – even a dog takes care of its stomach.

But we are human beings.

Along with ourselves, we have to do something for others, we have to brighten the lives of others, we have to spread happiness on every crying face, we have to contribute in fulfilling the dreams of every mother's son and once, then we have to contribute whatever we can to make India a golden bird. Again.

So get up, think and decide whether you want to be a part of other's network or make people a part of your network?

You can also do if you also want to make your net worth crores in the next five to ten years, then tie the knot that no one else will help you except the network indies.

For some companions who keep moving forward like a continuous river stream. If there is a problem in the middle of the cup, then by ripping the difficulties' scapula, we keep moving forward and one day we reach our destination.

And everything seemed unaccountable,
   Don't worry about that and you
   Don't stare the floor for a jiffy
   Just don't dare everyone,
   accept it in peace,
   The only thing that the heart should know,
   This moment will pass
   Don't lose your dreams
   Never sleep without doing it,
   You will also get the destination,
   If you keep growing every moment,
   You too will be successful .

4

Rajesh Kumar Thakur - Victory is important

Thank you for the love you guys got for writing my network marketing experience in short words.! Special Thanks to my younger brother Sanjeev Prajapati. Thanks to the one who gave me the way to make my idea come true.

I am sharing some of my experience in network marketing. Note this point down. What and how to do network marketing

1. Don't make it a hobby, make it a habit.
2. Bring change in your thinking, Bring change in your life
3. If the offline line motivates you , then change the track.
4. Know that you will win only by fighting the battle.

Details ahead:::::::::: !!!!!

Details of Network Marketing and How to do it

I try to give you some reasons that you can set a straight path by making it your target. Those people who do network marketing have three major dreams.

Expensive Car

Luxury Bungalow

Economic Freedom

To summarize, you are engaged in network marketing, which has three main benefits that will motivate you to work towards achieving your dreams within a specific time frame. Setting goals and working towards them is crucial for success in this industry. If you can fulfill these three dreams within the specified time frame, 70% of your work is done. The remaining 30% is to learn how to achieve success in network marketing.

To put it simply, many people don't understand the basic concept of marketing, which is creating a group of customers in order to sell products or ideas. With network marketing, instead of relying on one person to use a product or idea to its fullest potential, a group of people can use it for shorter periods of time, resulting in more work and more income. This is why network marketing is a good business and can lead to wealth.

1) Don't make it a hobby, make it a habit

To use an analogy, habits are like rain – they fall and flow everywhere, but they settle and stay in a pond where there is no disturbance. Similarly, bad habits won't go away unless you actively work to replace them with good habits. You can't expect success in network marketing if you don't make it a part of your daily routine and lifestyle. Success in this business requires consistency and persistence, and making it a habit is crucial. Don't treat it like a mere hobby that you can do occasionally; rather, incorporate it into your daily habits to ensure success.

2) Change your thinking - Change your life

If you're involved in network marketing and change your mindset, you'll always stand out in society and move in a positive direction. Network marketing is unique in that it constantly challenges and expands your thinking, and embracing it can transform your life. The opportunity to develop a positive mindset and find your purpose is unparalleled in network marketing. By making a habit of attending training meetings, seminars, reading motivational books, and practicing positive thinking, you can cultivate your excitement and move closer to success day by day. So, take the time to study this book on network marketing and keep striving towards your goals – one day, you will achieve them.

3) If the offline line motivates you, then change the track.

In the business you are involved in, it is likely that someone above you in the hierarchy is available online. And as you continue working, you will face some challenges. It's important to understand that difficulties are a part of any work you do. However, in this case, you should write down those difficulties in your notebook and share them with your senior. If your senior cannot provide a proper answer, these difficulties will continue to affect your work and may cause failure.

You may experience restlessness and lack of peace for a while, but if your motivation does not work and you feel disappointed, there is no need to despair. You can either change your senior or switch to a different track as much as possible.

4) Know that you will win only by fighting the battle

Defeat is not important in life. If you want to shine in the world of network marketing, then you have to burn like the sun. Every day something or the other happens in front of your eyes, but people do not pay attention because we are ignorant. Every day something or the other is teaching us that we will have to fight to win..!

A small example. There were main characters in Mahabharata, from which the important character of Karna Katha, Lord

Krishna knew that he could not win Arjuna war with Karna, along with fighting the battle, knowledge is also important and after fighting the battle, Arjuna won the war on the strength of knowledge.... .

This victory is important, if you go to work in films, you will find many negative people, you will find people who break your morale, it is a war for you, if you win then you will get 100% success..!

That's why victory is important.

5

Aman Kumar - Need for direct selling in present times

We spend our time and money working in companies like robots from 9 to 6. Despite living in the modern era, our lives are full of struggles. We invest in our jobs and then live in fear of spending our money. This is the reality of 21st century humans. We call it "Ziggy." Even if we receive promotions, salary increases, or pensions, we still may not feel happy. We often blame the results of our work or language barriers for our dissatisfaction and create our own comfort zones, much like frogs in a well.

We simplify this truth by considering the well as our world. We don't want to go to the sea. Some of the reasons for this are as follows –

- We do not consider ourselves worthy of the sea.
- We do not know how to cross the sea.
- We give the respect of sea to the well.

To gain a better understanding of ourselves, we should consider joining network marketing even if we feel undeserving of bigger things. It can provide us with the tools to find our way to success. If we settle for less, it only shows our limited thinking. We need to either step out of our comfort zone and challenge ourselves or we will remain stagnant and become a burden to society. We tend to focus solely on making money, disregarding our personal growth, and this has become our purpose in life.

It is possible for us to live a happy and fulfilling life with economic independence and mental stability if we choose to. However, if we do not want to live like modern-day animals in the 21st century, we must have come across the concept of network marketing at some point.

Study - Degree - Job - Earn - Spend - Die

Network Marketing: A Game

From my point of view network marketing is a game. A game in which you have to move forward fearlessly and in the same proportion your energy, your health, your bank balance and your team also increase, that is, this game becomes easier.

The one who understood the basic rules of this game is called the people of the pinnacle of this game i.e. the winner.

1. Being a listener means listening to people's nonsense
2. Keep to stand on your ground in any situation.
3. Keep learning from your mistakes.

These are some of the basic rules of this game which make you the winner of this game.

You do not need any loan, any debt etc. to start this business. You just need to know how to handle money and if you learn to stand your ground in any situation then you can become the king of network marketing.

Network Marketing?

Other people are often anxious about their jobs, working long hours and becoming mentally unwell. They may strive in the wrong direction, expecting a different result but end up in despair. However, network marketing is a business that doesn't require working long hours, as you are your own boss and can work at any time, either full-time or part-time.

You can also allocate time for your family in this business. This enhances your mood and keeps you mentally balanced. Network Marketing is presently the only business that fully takes charge of your development. You continuously improve your person-ality in this business, which is a defining feature of successful individuals. By engaging in this business, your life improves in all aspects, including your health, your relationships, your personality, and your business. Your promotion is constantly progressing.

Network marketing can provide you with financial stability, enhance your career opportunities and teach you how to make connections, which can lead to a happier personal life. The larger your network, the greater your net worth. Given the current inflationary period, I believe that network marketing is the most secure path to achieving financial independence. As we start building our network and connecting with people, our network grows and we obtain an economic network.

Future of network marketing

If we talk about the future, if there is a lot of opportunities in any business, then it is network marketing.

Unemployment and poverty are prevalent issues in Indian society, but there will come a time when they will no longer be insurmountable with the help of network marketing. Even students can participate in network marketing and earn valuable experience while still in school, which will benefit them in their future careers. Network marketing is a field full of opportunities for people of all types, and with the advent of social media, it has the potential to spark a revolution. The key to success in network marketing is to have a passion for it and remain committed to your goals.

6

MIS Ahmed - What is Multi Level Marketing

hat is multi level marketing?

W To many, multi-level marketing is perceived as a scheme that involves recruiting and trapping people into a network. However, I disagree with this perception as it is a business that offers time and financial freedom, teaches valuable life skills, and can completely transform one's lifestyle. It is a system that operates with complete autonomy and allows for unlimited income potential with minimal investment, making it accessible to individuals with various levels of education. Whether one is educated or not, multi-level marketing offers a platform for achieving big dreams, making it the most advantageous system in the world.

Can Network Marketing be taken up as a career?

Answer is yes.

When it comes to choosing a career, many options come to our mind, but we usually only consider jobs, businesses, or professions. These options are often suggested to us by others. However, I believe that limiting ourselves to these options can result in losing sight of our high ambitions and dreams. Unique methodical multi-level marketing offers an alternative career path that can provide unlimited financial opportunities, freedom from stress, and respect. By investing a limited amount of money and time, one can achieve financial stability and success.

In the modern times, leaders have revealed a secret that the value of this industry is greater than other industries as it provides happiness, peace and contentment that cannot be attained even after spending a lifetime and a lot of money. Currently, I am involved in multi level marketing where honest business practices lead to success. This business doesn't require a large amount of capital or excessive education, and the benefits extend beyond just financial earnings. It brings about an overall positive change that is much needed in today's society. Multi level marketing is the ultimate career of this century that has no barriers such as age, caste, religion, education or any kind. Its core principle is "Give success and get success."

Currently in India, there is a growing trend of young people pursuing Multi Level Marketing Business, which is helping to reduce unemployment. This business provides an opportunity to not only earn money and gain recognition through hard work and honesty, but also to help fulfill the dreams of millions of people.

Multi level Marketing Business provides a career opportunity as it is easy to enter and offers vast economic possibilities. It is similar to other professions such as being a doctor, engineer, or I.P.S. However, to succeed in this field, one must work hard and be consistent for at least five years. One should also avoid falling for new temptations, such as joining greedy companies or following the wrong leaders. It is like digging ten feet each in ten different places; even after digging a hundred feet, we may not find water. However, by focusing our energy on one place, we can dig forty to fifty feet and find water. Similarly, by dedicating five years to Multi level Marketing, one can build a successful career for life. Today, network marketing is expanding globally and is looking for individuals with dreams, ambition, a commercial mindset, and leadership abilities to join the field and achieve economic and social security. Those who oppose or are unsuccessful in network marketing business may not have understood its true nature. Network marketing is a legitimate business where products and sales are involved. The only difference is that a common person works hard and earns little for themselves, but in network marketing, they can earn a significant income and fulfill their big dreams by becoming a great person. Therefore, it is a wise decision to choose network marketing as a career.

The biggest risk is not to take a risk... In this world that is changing really fast, the only strategy that is bound to fail is not to take a risk.

13 Best Tips for Success in Network

Marketing | Top 13 Network Marketing Tips for Success

Establishing a network marketing enterprise may provide a profitable method to acquire supplementary income or even become your primary revenue stream. Nonetheless, identifying where to commence may seem bewildering for many who express interest in network marketing. Yet, by concentrating on establishing one business and duplicating profitable techniques, you can prevent feeling inundated and unclear. Merely putting in additional effort does not ensure success, therefore, it is vital to adhere to guidance from those who have already accomplished success in network marketing. By implementing these initial methods, you can swiftly commence your business and begin earning extra income for yourself and your loved ones.

1. (Reputation)

Have you ever tried to limit the creative ideas of entrepreneurs in a business opportunity and still managed to make a considerable profit? However, it is important to note that the techniques used in previous opportunities may not necessarily work for a new business venture, hence the need to conduct thorough research before committing to it. It is natural to be careful about the potential risks involved when there is no evidence of previous success in making money from the opportunity.

2. Capturing Non-viable Mothers

(Holding Non-Vibrant Benefits)

To make your profession productive and thriving, it's important to avoid being anxious or bothered by it, as it affects your communication with others. If you don't have full confidence in yourself and your abilities, others won't either. It's important to be skilled in network marketing or any other related field, but if your confidence is lacking, your business may fail.

Because you're the leader, everything starts with you!

3. Planning direct Tip

(direct Selling Tips of Making Plans)

It is widely known that network distributors work from home, which means they often overlook the need for a planner. You can use various tools like notebooks, calendars on your laptop, or phone to manage your time effectively. If you want to improve your time management skills, you can refer to Stephen Covey's book "The Seven Habits of Highly Effective People." To plan your day efficiently, it is recommended that you prepare the night before, so that you are ready to work the next day. Here are some helpful tips: stick to your plans.

4. Setting Goals

To start with outdoor marketing, it is important to have a clear plan in any particular niche to increase your chances of success. Some people may attempt this business without setting goals and lose hope when they don't meet their expectations. By setting specific and achievable goals, you increase your chances of success. However, it is important to avoid making unrealistic commitments that can lead to failure if not met. Instead, focus on developing practical and effective strategies. While determination is essential, it is also important to take the time to prepare your goals thoroughly.

5. Home-Based Business Ages of Continuing Learning

(Home-Based Business Tips Continuing Learning)

To be successful in network marketing, it is important to have a good understanding of the industry, the company you are working with, and the products you are selling. Stay updated on current events and be prepared to answer questions about your business. Avoid speaking negatively about others, as it can reflect poorly on your character and business ethics. Stay open to learning and continue to educate yourself about the industry. Don't wait too long to take action, as opportunities may pass by if you delay too much.

6. Proper Mind Setting

business and be heard by everyone. How about moving up the ladder instead of falling when you can try it? I find out Before getting started in the networking business, you have to get the right mindset. This means setting aside all negativity to create knowledge on the way to success in this.

7. Lessons from the Referral Business Ticket to Listen

(Referral Business Tips of Learn how to listen)

It is not only an important life learning but also an important business skill. The sponsoring distributors will be trained to listen and the experience of the first months to determine people's desires will be easy. We are not trying to every living organism within 5 feet of people to develop financial profit from our opportunity. For those of you who have already become a referral business company, the guidance here will realize that there are some contradictions. It is hoped that this was not a strategy that was dictated in the initial months.

8. MLM Business Tips of Being a Business Leader

(MLM Business Tips of Being a Business Leader)

You need the leadership skills you need to lead by example and demonstrate to others on your business team. Attend all events, seminars, video conferences, meetings and training. When you don't, why doesn't anyone on your team? As a business leader, you need to be an expert and need to be copied by others to learn about MLM business success. Understand that you are gaining, therefore, you will learn in a different way than by the repetition method.

9. Growth rate network business letter

(Network Business Tips of Growth Rate)

When it is a network business opportunity, you will undoubtedly need to control the rate of growth. Is the product sustainable in the long term and is the consumer more of a focal point than developing this way? This can be one of the important factors related to the opening of any network business opportunity.

10. Consider it as Business

Network Marketing has become absolutely huge popularity among the top entrepreneurs of the world. These top entrepreneurs are ready to achieve the success of this network business and the secret behind this is that they really want to start their business as a real business. needed to be used and did it with gusto. You can group the business together as unreliable as the same business unit.

It should be pursued with a strong passion and not just as a hobby. One theory that a lot of entrepreneurs have is a misconception, on the issue that businesses require very little investment and that a lot of us consider to be whimsical. That is, however, they are not ready to set themselves up to be a network marketer to be successful.

11. NETWORK BUSINESS ADVENTURES OF SELECT MINDS

(Network Business Tips of Select Mentor)

As in most popular sports, there is a coach at the back to teach and direct the team. To make network business success, it is strongly advised to select gurus from the up-line of your business team. An upline network business team leader who has successfully achieved business achievements will be your most effective guide. You recommend him to teach you as a guru. Then most of what they say they do! Bolo chalo and a tremendous success yatra is waiting for you to be successful.

12. The direct Tip of Patience

(Direct Selling Tips of Having Patience)

Direct business is not a fancy theme it is a realistic slowly operative business; That's why it takes effort, motivation, training and dedication to be successful. No success ever comes overnight.   1 or 2 to get optimum financial benefit.   It will take years, and then you will be able to leave the current job. Therefore, meeting any duty with patience is inward.

13. Never Quit

No matter what obstacles you encounter, you never want to quit. You will only fail during this business trip while you stand aside to quit. As it says, "Never a winner, but never a loser". Always remember this for the journey to business success. So, never, never, never leave. Hence, the above recommended network marketing strategies will prove useful to achieve the goals and objectives to sustain in this industry to make your networking organization successful.

How to get success in MLM Business ?

In our country, education is widely pursued, but not everyone can secure employment. As a result, people seek out alternative ways to earn money. Many individuals have turned to network marketing or MLM as a means of generating income, with some achieving great success. It is important to understand what it takes to succeed in this field, so that we too can achieve success. In this article, we will delve into the details of MLM, providing insights on how to achieve success in this business.

Before joining an MLM business, it's essential to gather complete information about the company. You can easily access information with the help of technology, so don't blindly trust any company. Investigate every aspect of the company, such as its history, location, and founders. Find out if the company is registered with the government or not. Also, take feedback from people who are already involved in the business.

Understand the knowledge under which work is done in the company. Unless you understand the knowledge properly, you will not be able to do the work properly. After understanding the plan, if you feel that you will be able to do that work, then only join it.

After signing up, socialize with the people associated with it and everyone Try to learn the working style. make friends with as many people as possible .

When you add your subordinates, choose such people who are active and completely dedicated to work.

Keep motivating your team from time to time and encourage them for the work they do, this will make your team more active and the interest among people about the work will also increase.

Talk to those people who have reached high places in your company and get information about all the work from them. Try to learn from them how they worked and achieved success.

Never tell wrong things to others, do not lie, tell only what is the truth.

Because the foundation of lies is hollow, if you lie once then no one will trust you again.

Reach out to people and encourage them to work. Explain the plan to the people in this way. So that it is easy for people to connect with the company and enjoy working.

How to choose Multi Level Marketing (MLM) company?

You will get success in MLM business only when you do the work yourself but the most important thing is to have the right company to work for. Because if the company is not good then there is no use of working. Let us know how to choose the right company.

As I have already told that it is very important to identify the company and take all its information. First of all, know that when the company was formed and how old is it? Total how many people have joined in this. Who is the manager of the company?

Who is the leader of the company, meet and talk to him and

get information about how to earn in this?

Never join without visiting the company's office and site yourself. There is no dearth of fake and fuzz workers, that's why the more careful you are, the more it comes.

Find out about the mother of the company you want to join. Checking his legal document by himself. It is mandatory to be the official mother of the company, never join such a company which does not have legal document or else they do not want to show their papers. Such people only cheat you

Try to get complete information about the plan.

Also know whether the membership plan is onetime or it is renewed annually.

Also take information about the consorship. Get the company code information and know the income ratio

Formula to build a great team.

What do people do more?   After joining, they make a team and after making a team, they start working. don't learn first you have to learn from your upline from your company's top achiever leader you have to learn from them then after learning you have to make your own team till you make your own team you will not go out to work then Till then you will never be able to become a great leader.

I am telling you, you can make your team big. Because you don't have to do the work And one thing to be aware of is that when people join, after that when they go to show their knowledge, some people immediately talk negatively about them. So that they get demotivated somewhere and secondly when they look towards their upper line. When a team of thousand two thousand, 10000 people is attached there, then they get worried that how will I connect so many people, then both of you do not need to worry. If you work under the formula I yourself. You have to get it done and you have to do it together with them.

As in today's time every mobile phone uses email and when mobile phone is used, it also has a lot of social media apps downloaded, such as WhatsApp, Facebook, etc.

I have to share my knowledge with those people and take your upper line for support and show your knowledge, when you show your knowledge again and again, you will also understand where you are doing wrong. By this you will understand. Some people must have joined you within this 1 month.

Because the number you have, at least 100 200 numbers in the phone, then everyone keeps keeping up with you, you just have to reach those 100 people. When you have done this then all you have to do is teach this to your team and see how your team does after that. Because when the 1st lower leader joins one, then there will be two, after that their totals will be the same as yours. Now we just have to start working together with them. If you wanna go for a single leg then you need one and if you wanna go for binary/matching then you need 2 if you it's matric then you need 3 people or 5 people.

Should You can make a big team just by teaching this team.

We do this only at 12 o'clock. Everyone who joins has to be doubled. Let's assume that you have added 2 people, now only two of those two have to join, with the help of all, you and your upline will be included in the help.

Such as:-

hey = team
1 = 2
2 = 4
3 = 8
4 = 16
5 = 32
6 = 64
7 = 128
8 = 256
9 = 512
10 = 1024
11 = 2048
12 = 4096

In 12 weeks, how much was the total team of 8190 people, if we convert 12 weeks into months, then the total is 4 months, if we assume that you could not join in one month, then you will join in 1 week, but in 12 weeks you will become a bigger team. So don't be afraid, just focus, use both your time and your team's time properly.   And within no time you will become a great leader.

How much does it feel like listening to a JOB in English? A lot isn't it?*

but
   A job is spoken in Hindi which has a direct meaning.
   Servant
   Study till 12th and give 12 years of our life to study.
   After that 3 years graduation
   then 2 years

Master's degree for 17 years.

After that a company

You go for an interview.

After spending lakh of rupees in studies

A man sitting opposite decides that

How much salary will you get in a month.

Think 1 thing that only you have spent money for your studies.

So who is that person sitting in front of you who is going to charge you?

How much salary should he give?

It's not your fault either of you

where exactly do you live, your parents, your neighbors, people in your radar will put only one thing in your mind

That son, you have to study from here and do the same job.

Everyone has put this worm of job in your mind.

but

Think for once that what happens by doing a job?

You give 10 hours out of 24 hours of your day to your boss and take around 10000 rupees from him.

Some take 15000 rupees by giving 14 hours a day.

It clearly means that you are selling your time.

You give a profit of 1 lakh to your boss, then you get about 10 thousand rupees.

Simple maths: you only get back about 10% of your hard work.

thousands of people are like you

If you use it for yourself, then can't you become a millionaire?

job seeker always compromises himself. Neither is there a bike. There is no car.

No home either. No vacation. Nor is there a stimulant happy life.

The job says only one thing.

I will not let you die of hunger

We were born poor, it is not our fault.

But dying poor would be the biggest sin.

Prime Minister of our country

Narendra Modi ji also speaks.

If you work, you too can fulfill all your dreams.

direct selling is the fastest growing business of the 21st century.

There are 4 types of top leadership qualities.

- Dreams
- Dedication & Discipline
- Delegation
- Daring

(Dreams)

Those people are alive in the world who have dreams. First of all you have to see that you have dreams if you don't then because you must have mostly seen that the one who does not have dreams, when he wakes up the next day, he does not know what he has to do?

When there are no dreams, there is no plan, when there is no plan, you will not do anything, you spend all your time in this thinking and you would have wasted your whole life like this. So from today the first thing you will do is that you will see dreams and when you see dreams, now a goal will be ready for you to fulfill it. Now you have dreams then to fulfill dreams we will keep working till the dream come true.

Dedication & Discipline

Every day people make a knowledge and keep making knowledge, it happens that they can never implement like people make knowledge of morning walk that from tomorrow I will go for morning walk, from today I will go for morning walk but general only It happens that people are not able to go out for morning walk, so unless you have the design and dedication inside you, you will not be able to complete any of your work completely.

The foundation of dreams depends only on your dedication and your discipline. Unless you have dedication and discipline towards your dreams, you will not be able to do that work.

Dedication means that no matter how much it rains, no matter how stormy it may be, no matter how cold it is, it may be hot, you have to forget about any kind of trouble you are facing and completely surrender yourself to the work you want to do. are thinking Yes.

Discipline As you must have seen that if there is no discipline in life then no work can be done on your time. I believe that if there is discipline then time is your money and if you waste your time then your money is wasted. Understood that in today's date, whatever work you do, if you give 8 hours, in that 8 hours, if you take some leave in between, then you understood that time is your loss or not, that money is your loss. If it is done, if discipline is not there, then the whole work is not concrete.

Similarly, see that if you do not come on time towards your work, then your junior behind you will also not be dedicated towards his work. If any leader himself does not become responsible for his work, then he can never dedicate any of his energetic syndication below for his work. So if his team's time is bad then your time is wasted. This means if your money is lost, you will have to be dedicated, your team will have to be dedicated, the team will be dedicated after seeing how disciplined you are.

You have to set this example to your team like K. Narayana-muthy ji who is the owner of Infosys. The way he did it was whenever he went to his campus when he saw someone

If there is any garbage lying anywhere in the corner, then he used to go and throw it in the garbage day and everyday he used to do this in this way, his whole team, when his staff saw that in this way, Sir was doing it.

Our leader chooses the one who looks stronger than him, has better quality than him, has better knowledge inside him, so if you have better knowledge inside than your down line, then only you will be able to become a strong and a great leader. First of all, you have to bring all that fault within yourself, you have to see whether I, as a leader, can make my team do all these things, make them achieve, make them earn income, make them do better work. Whether it is one leader, whether it is 10 leaders or 2000 leaders, leadership is a quality, you can take your team far ahead, you will earn yourself and they will also earn. I do not say that you should not give time to your family. Don't give time to both of you. You don't make your girlfriend, don't enjoy, don't listen to songs, don't do this and don't do that, do everything but when you sit to work, then full time you should be at work, like 1 minute if you If you worked then it should be in 10 minute increments like if you worked for 10 minutes then it should be in 1 hour increments like

If you worked for one hour, then it should be a full 8 hours of work. Means when I am sitting to work, then he is sitting to work and that work should be such that people should see and people should follow you.

1. Delegation

First of all, you should know how to give work, that is, you should know how to give responsibility. Now if you give responsibility under yourself, then your team will work, when your team will work then you can do anything. I am having fun with family, you have gone on vacation for 10 days, for 20 days and money is coming to you. All this will be possible when your team will be working under you. Is it that after giving the work to the team, they have to see how that work is being done? If the work is not going right, then you have to teach it, it is not that you have spoken once or twice and then sat down, you have to teach it again and again until it becomes like you, you have to make people like you, only then you can make a big group. Gay. The umpires will be able to stand tall only then you will be able to fulfill the dream of being a billionaire. If you have worked with discipline. If you have put yourself in full force, then only you will be able to do this work completely. It is the duty of every team leader to get the work done by his team, you see everywhere, no matter what sense he is in, like a manager, then the team is below him, then his work is below him, who is his team,

If you sit down to do everyone's work then you will repent and how long will you do it, you can never become big. It has to be done so that when he does it, he will learn and when he learns, he will become great himself and will make you great.

small drop of any color in a full bowl of water, then it makes the whole water in its own color, that is, it Bad It is the responsibility of every leader, every person sitting at the top, whether he is a manager, whether he is a leader, whether he is an owner, that he should make the team below him work and who does not work, then throw him out. does Must have seen that one non-functioning spoils the whole team. As you must have seen that if you put a changes it, so if there is anyone in your team who Not listening to him can spoil the whole team. Can spoil all your hard work. Pick it up and throw it out, uproot it, throw out the root which is spoiling your entire tree, spoiling your hard work, then you become a decision maker and you can take the decision only then you work.

2. Daring

Courage is very important word in your future if you are in a position to take courage. If you have the courage, then you are in a position to take decisions, and if you are in a position to take decisions, then you can do any work on a very large scale.

You have to take a decision, you can do any work only by decision. If any leader says that he has not taken any wrong decision in his life then leave him immediately because it means he never took courage and one who cannot take courage can never take decision who cannot take decision . He can never become a successful man. Never be afraid of taking decisions because the one who takes decisions is always successful. You must have seen when you cycled for the first time ever, you must have been hurt, you must have fallen, but after that you did not ride that cycle properly, you saw when you are getting down to bathe in the river and when you see If you didn't know how to swim up above your nose fills with water. If water fills in ear but after that you don't learn to swim then you have to take first decision to learn then only you will be able to work and work will be done only when you start you must have seen that no small leader grows up Can become because he is not fully learned, if he learns completely then only he becomes. You have seen those who have shown courage, like Dhirubhai Ambani ji is doing his business all over the world today, like you see, OYO's owners are worth crores at such a young age, and there are many more. Those who started a startup and today are on a very big stage, then if you have the courage. You are too shy to do anything

Time is not always the same.

Once, after becoming the President of South Africa, Nelson Mandela went to eat at a restaurant with his security personnel. Everyone ordered food of their choice and started waiting for the food to arrive.

At the same time, on the seat in front of Mandela's seat, one was waiting for his food. Mandela asked his security staff to invite him to his table as well. After the food arrived, everyone started eating, that man also started eating his food, but his hands were trembling while eating.

After eating the food, the man bowed his head and came out of the train.

After the man had left, Mandela's security officer told Mandela that he was probably very ill, that his food and hands were constantly trembling, and that he himself was trembling.

Mandela said no, it is not so. He was the jailer of the jail in which I was confined. Whenever I was tortured and I used to ask for water while moaning, he used to urinate on me.

Mandela said I have become a president now, he thought that I would probably treat him the same way. But mine is not like that. I think acting out of revenge leads to destruction. On the other hand, the mentality of patience and tolerance leads us towards development.

To become a good networker, you always have to consider your team as your family, then you will see that at what point your team takes you, always successful can be successful only with your team, never alone, otherwise you will treat the team like your family and earn money yourself and the team less than anyone else.

If someone makes a mistake, don't think of taking revenge from him, just forget him because time is not always the same. Despair is your world. This article is for those leads who have become #Network _ Marketing disappointment due to one reason or the other, and are now away from this beautiful industry. Both fail when you give up trying one more time while great success always comes after great difficulties. That's why if you are repeatedly failing to achieve any of your goals, it means that your goal is more special and important, that's why it is not being fulfilled easily.

Amitabh Bachchan's first super hit film was before Zanjeer.

17 consecutive films were Super Flops.

Thomas Alva Edison invented Bulb after failing yoga 9999 times. Got success in inventing the 10,000th time.

Mr. KR Narayana Murthy, before founding Infosys in 1981,

had tried unsuccessfully to set up a company called Softronics in 1976.

Tata Indica Car Launched by Ratan Tata in 1998 Failed had to say-Chairman of Ford Company showed interest in buying Tata Indica Plant but his behavior with Ratan Tata was quite insulting. Then decided to sell the entire plant of Indica. After many tries. No one wanted to buy this car. That's why Ratan Tata says,

"When you do not understand the Car Business, why try to do it."

After a few years, in 2008, the Jaguar-Land Rover of the same Ford Company proved to be a failed project and Ratan Tata bought the entire project of this Jaguar. This time the words of the Chairman of the same Ford Company said-

"You are doing us a favor by buying our company."

The founders of Ford Car making company had unsuccessfully tried to establish 5 more companies before Ford Company and Ford At the time of setting up the company, they were completely ruined financially.

Author of world's best selling novel, Harry Potter's JK Rowling was a modest waiteress and no publisher was ready to publish her novel. This novel could be published only because the 8-year-old daughter of its publisher begged her father to publish it and the publisher could not reject the request.

Famous Basketball Player, Michael Jordan wasn't even considered worth selecting.in his School Team

Albert Einstein could not even speak till the age of 4 and was a victim of a disease called Autism. But because of his mathematical and physics principles, modern science is measuring the distances of differences.

The experience of every successful person is that every failure is a step in the ladder of success.

So try one more time. Who knows, you may be standing at the last rung of your success ladder and this attempt may be your last attempt for success because if you fail 9999 times

Had Edison not tried his invention for the 10000th time, we might still be living under the light of a lamp or a chimney.

So don't give up, shoot...

Replace no to yes! Here's how?

As you must have seen, you will find many leaders who keep saying that love, I showed him knowledge, showed him knowledge, he did not connect, he did not connect and my work is not being done, friend. I am tired and upset. If France is not coming, then these five things have to be kept in mind for all of them, how to change Kana Ko Ham?

- Do not allow Na to enter your mind. When we go to show our knowledge to someone and there the person says no to us, then we get disappointed and we are disappointed because he said no whereas he just said no and did not say anything to you. Have not killed. Did not kill you. Now you were not shot, no such thing was done to you. From where you feel that you are lost, it was a word, he told you no, he speaks, I don't want to, then you will go to the second, go to the third. You will have to do it until you get the loss, if it comes, otherwise you will work on this policy, only then you will be able to succeed in level marketing.
- The knowledge you may have shown that there is some deficiency in your way of showing your knowledge, then correct that deficiency again and then show the knowledge

again, then he speaks, then it means that there is some deficiency again. Is there something in you in your way, something in him then right. Do it and go again until your presentation is done, if the person in front does not say yes to you, then you have to remove your shortcomings. Those shortcomings have to be rectified again. And then he has to go till his yes comes out.

- If yes still does not come out then now you have to do something different which till now no one else has been able to show your knowledge. Means you have to go to the depth of that knowledge. You have to go to the depth of the rod you are going to sell. You should know every minute detail of that road. How will a user benefit from it and in what way should he speak to others so that people can understand that way and connect with him. If you explain this thing to him very easily, he will connect with you immediately and will say yes immediately.

- If he still doesn't say yes, then you should show your income that people always want to hear. If you succeed in convincing them, then the boss will immediately say yes to you.

7

Kavita Bansal - Direct selling: A goldmine

We would like to have an important discussion with you today about achieving success. To achieve success, you need to possess five things – hard work, sacrifice, struggle, self-belief, and an unwavering determination. If you have all of these things, you can achieve all of your dreams, and live life on your own terms. It's time to think about the impossible things that you see around you today, and turn them into your dreams. Your dreams should be ambitious and big, because if you want to achieve something that you've never achieved before, you have to do something that you've never done before. With network marketing, you can work from anywhere, without any investment, name, fame, caste, height or beauty. By putting in effort and dedication, you can earn enough to buy a house and a car, and achieve financial freedom through multi-level marketing.

You may want to have additional income, economic stability for your own business, help others, gain peace of mind, personal growth, acquire knowledge, bring good fortune to your leaders, have job and time freedom. You have to make a decision now about your career. Remember that you cannot become wealthy by having a job, but by running a business. You can utilize not only your own skills but also the skills of others through the power of duplication. One person can only accomplish a hundred percent of work, but if you ask 100 people to do one percent of the work, it will be much easier. This is known as the power of networking, or by other names such as direct selling or network marketing. MLM is a marketing model that companies use to distribute their products and services among people. In MLM's direct or multi-level marketing, we sign up new people through phone calls and earn income for ourselves and our downline.

Everyone should follow the principles of Multi Level Marketing. By doing so, you can become wealthy and your name will be among the rich people in the world. To achieve this, you need to become a leader and help others become smart consumers. This will help you build your network and become a successful entrepreneur.

The marketing approach we use involves 20% focus on details and 80% on advertising. In the traditional system, the manufacturer sells to a middleman, who then sells to a wholesaler and then to a retailer. A lot of money is spent on advertising and the middlemen make a lot of profit. Our unique system eliminates these middlemen and the product goes directly from the manufacturer to the consumer, with the profit being split among us. This is similar to online shopping where the middleman is removed. Our goal is to create a network between the company and the customers, without any middlemen. This may seem like a daunting task, but we can accomplish it together as a team.

The starting point is always at zero, even the big players start simple, but their hard work and passion make them champions. It's important to remove ego and focus on the task at hand. You might be wondering how to make it happen and if you're capable of doing it, but remember that your upperline and winning team are ready to assist you in taking your business forward. All you need to do is follow their lead and the path they've laid out for you. Success comes from being part of a successful group with experienced leaders who can guide and support you in growing your business. Our winning team provides an education system to help you become a successful leader. We offer books, CDs, motivational and training meetings, seminars, and guidance on how to expand your business. Through development and leadership, we explain the business and help you achieve growth.

This book is designed to motivate you and propel you forward. By reading it, you will gain valuable insights and confidence to advance your business. This bestseller provides practical guidance on how to become wealthy, and according to Kavita Bansal, investing is the real key to wealth creation. Although hard work is necessary, the fruits of labor are always rewarding. By persevering and staying focused, you can achieve great success and reach new heights.

This is the network marketing of the 21st century that is emerging today. It is a business plan that allows you to have flexibility in your schedule. Always remember that to have the best days, you must push through the bad days, such as during an epidemic like COVID-19 or during economic instability. During such times, when it's hard to find a job, you can sit at home and still do business with something that's on the growth side. Network marketing is a business that you can do from home, and you can do it for just two hours a day. It's best to solve your own problems rather than depending on others. If you're ready to change your life, we're here to support you, and you can contact us for help.

This book can provide you with more information about the emerging business of the 21st century, which is direct network marketing. By understanding this business model, you can transform your life and achieve your dreams, big or small. As the saying goes, "There are thousands of ways for the rich to become rich but there is only one way for the poor to become rich, that is direct." Network marketing is like growing a crop that takes time to bear fruit, but if you keep at it, you will eventually see results. The network marketing market has spread all over the world, and you can make a difference and achieve success in life. As the quote goes, "If you can't get up then try to run, if you can't run then walk, if you can't walk then crawl but just keep going." When asked about their preferred career field, successful entrepreneurs like Bill Gates and Donald Trump have expressed their interest in network marketing, which indicates the potential and growth of this business in the future.

You can begin a network marketing business with no upfront investment and start earning passive income. It's a great business opportunity that allows you to travel and develop yourself while generating income. The future belongs to network marketing because traditional government jobs are disappearing, and not everyone has the ability to start their own business. Network marketing is the only option left for many people, and everyone should consider entering this field to secure their financial future. Your success in this field will depend on your efforts and ability to generate income. If you find this information helpful, please share it with others so that more people in India can learn about the benefits of network marketing.

Expand your perspectives and don't restrict yourself. Success is just a little further away, and with a team of committed individuals, the leader's success is the team's success. Build yourself up like a tree that provides shade and fruits, don't attempt to alter the direction of the wind as it's beyond your control. Instead, change your path and approach to brighten your family's future with fresh and innovative ideas. Keep working diligently because when you undertake any task with determination, thorough preparation, and persistent effort, the circumstances will be favorable to you. A great team will take you to the pinnacle of success and the season of failure is the ideal moment to sow the seeds of success since the new ideas created after failure can lead to success, and the seeds of those ideas are impervious to destruction.

To achieve success, it is important to understand that failure is merely a stepping stone towards it. Just like a tender plant is born from a tree, success is born from failure. Failure is actually success standing on its head. Having hopes and desires in one's heart is important to achieve something. It is crucial to work to earn income and manage expenses. However, if circumstances prevent one from working, income will cease to come in. Therefore, it is essential to earn money even from expenses. For example, if a shopkeeper can earn from your expenses on buying goods, then why not you? You can change the shop and save money while earning money at the same time. Hard work is the key to open the doors to a brighter future. Don't give up until you achieve the world's biggest income.

If you continue to do the same things, you will continue to get the same results. Some people talk about their salary while others talk about their turnover. If you have big dreams, you will need to put in a lot of effort. Although work is temporary, the recognition you receive from it will last. Hard work is the key to success.

In essence, the point is to comprehend the core of business, which is not just a trade, but a blend of safeguarding consumers. You are not simply buying a product for a low price, but investing in an establishment with multiple merits. This is a powerful concept that can elevate consumers to great heights and brighten their future, but it requires effort and dedication to build and sustain it.

To achieve success, you must understand that it requires effort and hard work, and that using your talents is crucial. Quitting before achieving victory is a sure way to lose. The path of least resistance is not always the right one, and it's important to choose your own path. You know yourself better than anyone else, so trust yourself. We hope that this article has provided you with valuable insights. If you have any questions, please don't hesitate to contact me. You should have understood how to invite people into network marketing by now. So, instead of being a consumer, become a business owner.

The work of network marketing has been our long-standing commitment. By practicing network marketing, you can bring yourself forward. To make a difference, you must first change yourself, as changing the world begins with changing oneself. Leaders who are capable of taking responsibility and making decisions, who are committed to moving forward, are followed by the majority of people. To become one of them, you must walk a different path and accomplish what others consider impossible. Success, not revenge, is what you should strive for. Success will change your life, and if you encounter any problems in life, rather than dwelling on them, focus on overcoming them. The bigger the dream, the greater the obstacles, but with persistence and hard work, success will come. It's time to start a new life by treating ourselves as we would others.

"Those who are fond of winning do not fear losing, because now I am my own coach"

8

Kesharam Kumawat - How To Have Basic Success In Network Marketing

irect selling - Beginning of a Viral Era - Till now we all have heard that the means of earning money is earned only by doing job, agriculture, or small business, but now the time is coming. There will be a big change in the market.

- Change with time- Friends, today's era is a very fast-paced era. Today, if we do not change with the times, then there will be a break in our business because now i.e. the business of the 20th century is direct (network marketing). Yes you heard right. direct is one such business which spreads like a virus. As I explain to you with an example. Just like how fast the corona virus spreads, similarly this business spreads at a fast pace. Similarly direct has also started like a viral in today's era.

- It has become necessary to change business along with this changing era of the 20th century. Because in the market even the small shops are now into big malls

- Unemployment is increasing due to full citation in the job also, that's why the working style will have to be changed. Both if we do not change with time then our life gets affected. Let me explain you with an old saying. For example, in the olden days, the strongest vehicle used to drive, which was very strong. High-ranking politicians, officials, and VIPs used to walk around but with time they did not convert their system into a heterological system. If the demand of the market was not recognized then both those vehicles are not in the market today. That's why the changing business of the coming 20th century is just like this direct. Yes, network marketing is the same. In this too, the fastest growing business is wellness

- Now there is a change in the food-drinking lifestyle of man. In olden times, food used to provide as much strength or let me say (as much nutrition). It is not available in today's food and hard work is not common because it is the era of technology, that's why my personal suggestion is to work in wellness industry. Due to which you get success. If I talk about me, then I used to work as a medical fish counter for a long time in a medical i.e. hotel, and due to the change in my lifestyle and eating habits, my obesity increased a lot and I took the nutrition and I got rid of obesity. When I came, people started asking me and I started telling, so that I started moving ahead in this field as soon as I saw it, and then I attended a seminar, so my vision about this industry came and I started within no time, in the first 6 months, my income started increasing to 25-30,00. In my spare time, I saw how much I could earn if I did this business full time. I asked myself this and got my answer.

I worked for about 6 years in a nutrition company and now my network marketing has changed not due to that.

I thank you from the bottom of my heart only my life but also the lives of many people along with me.

Do direct Selling or Network Marketing?

Let's look at the rising figures of rising inflation and rising prices. I will explain you through a table, if you understand this table correctly, then you will immediately decide to work in network marketing.

1940-10 .

1960-100 .

1980-1000 .

2000-10000 .

2020-1 lakh.

2040- 10 lakhs.

This is a researched data which states that

In the year 1940 – the family used to live in joint means, despite having a large number of people in one family 10. A month used to be spent, then the decade of 20 years came to an end, after that the year 1960-100. Fewer people started living in a few families, yet the monthly expenses increased from 10 to 100. Done.

Year 1980-1000 .- At this time few people in the family started living less. Still the monthly expenses started increasing i.e. at this time the average is 1000. Monthly expenses are required.

Year 2000-10000 .- A little more families kept getting smaller but the monthly expenses kept on increasing because from here the technology era started and inflation kept on increasing, now you must have understood that I want to explain.

Year 2020-1 lakh .

In this age, we are 2 of us, because of our expenses increasing so much, if you remain a small family in a small way, then they must need 1 lakh rupees per month because children's education, mobile expenses, car expenses, house The cost of all this together should be so much if you want to lead a decent life.

So I request you do you have any means to earn 1 lakh rupees. If your answer is no then you should start working in Wellness Network Marketing from today itself.

Is everyone's time and income running side by side? Like every man 1 lakh. Today's time is not earning for a month, then think how to reach 10 lakhs in the coming 2040, that's why we have to start the business of an era.

What are the means to earn 1 lakh rupees in today's era

1. Agriculture - 1 lakh per farmer. month earns?
2. Job
3. Business

In trade, there is an inward demand. I will tell you the means to work in traditional business and direct, from here you will take 100% decision, I have full faith.

Now you must have understood that in today's fast-paced era, along with rising inflation, if there is only one platform to increase our income, it is wellness industry.

In network marketing, wellness should be done indie only.

World's best economist Paul Jane predicts every time before the world revolution i.e. any market revolution. And his predictions are accurate. I'll tell you quickly.

Babies born between 1946-1964

Year 1950-1960 – Baby foods & Diapers (the business of food and clothes for babies). Those who did this business earned a lot of money at that time.

1970-1980 - worked in the generation real estate

People earned a lot of money, this third prediction was born by him.

1980-1990 – People who worked in the electronics market in this decade Did those people earn a lot of money at that time.

1990-2000 – Paul Zane predicted about this decade that the business of scooters will spread rapidly in the coming times and this is what you all know that those who did business in the field of scooters in this decade people made big money

Year 2000-2100 – For the time that is going on now, for this time, he has already predicted that the most fast and long-lasting business that will run is wellness industry and don't think about this statement from today. Do it

The biggest specialty of this business is that it can be started with very less capital. And the second specialty is that those who teach in this business remain moist for you. And in the second business i.e. the traditional business-shop, mall, job etc. no one is going to teach and in this business very educated and cunning people are going to teach you. That's why this type of business spreads very fast like a virus.

This industry i.e. network marketing is mothered by the government, in earlier times there was no guideline for network marketing in India, but in recent times, guidelines have also been issued by Government and the Prime Minister of our country also says that create employment. Most of all this business has come because you are your own boss. And you can do this business anytime anywhere.

There is an end to unemployment in the country. Unemployment increased with the changing times.

Lack of employment due to changing times and technological era and even if a job is available, today in the time of such inflation, the empty need is fulfilled by jobs and small businesses. But humans cannot fulfill their dreams just by that.

I would also request unemployed friends to look at this business and understand that if you start by taking training of this business with low cost, then I have full faith that you can change your life by doing network marketing business.

- In network marketing with which company to work - come and understand

- let's understand it in some detail. First of all, in my opinion, there should be a product base. You have to know in advance that the company is not selling any frames, dials or any premiums. Because without products the work can be like this. That's why you need to know this. And you should join the company of such brands whose products are in demand and trend oriented, you should give all this information.

Because you have made your goal to become a millionaire through network marketing, which can be fulfilled by your only effort. And the decision you have taken is the best and wisest decision. According to me there is a lot of demand for wellness based products in wellness industry in network marketing

- Is. Now this is the right time to work in this industry because although I have repeated you in the previous page, yet once again tells I tell you that in today's time due to change in food habits and lifestyle of people, many are getting busy. That's why there will be a lot of depression in the market of wellness products and if there is a lot of depression then it will be easy for you to do business and you will easily reach your destination .

- It is important to pay attention to special topics-
- Profile of the company.
- Information about company's products.
- Company's business knowledge
- About company's education system. 5.

What is Company's current status?

1. Company's Profile

Where is the company from? Who is the owner of company? What is company's mission? What is the vision of company, with company i.e. who are the scientists of the products, how much experience the owner of company has in network marketing, after knowing all this you should work with company.

2. Company's Roads

available with many company's in the market- Like: – In my opinion my story tells Indian in my wellness Indian company's products should be unique and there should be demand for that products in the market and it is easy to work in company's which are not working with previous company and is unique in which I am working. He and there are very few teams like companies and it is easy for me and everyone in the team to work. And resurrection is also taking place. In today's time life-style is being resolved and with whom I am is working on solving such a problem so you can too.

3. Company's business knowledge

Company's business knowledge is a must watch for you. Is there anything hidden in company's knowledge? Is it not in company's plan that the people at the top get profit and the people at the bottom get less profit? You should see all this information and it is also necessary to see whether it is not as if something is going wrong and about the distribution of the money with some more practical knowledge. There is a need to keep these books. When and how much money is being distributed to the deductees. And on what basis is she distributing the money. It is not that the company is based on money circulation. Because such companies are going to sell multi product in the market, that's why the products should work in the base company only. Let me tell you that the company is giving money according to the sale i.e. (turnover) of the products, then such company can be called right. If it is not distributing money on the turnover and is doing the work of money circulation, then understand that it is baseless and stay away from such companies.

4. C ompany's Education System

It is also very important to know whether the company in which you are going to work has an education system or not, if so, does your company have training once or twice a month or not. Because you can become a successful networker only when you attend the very best training. Training is very important to get success in network marketing. And it's important to see. Because you will get complete information about company from this and information about roads and how to avoid, how to get ridge and how to heal oven, you get to learn all this from education system only, that's why company's It is necessary to know the educational system.

5. Company's current rates

Is it possible that the market in which you are going to work is bad at present, or the products of that company are not showing any interest, or most of the people in that company are not earning money? Must be obtained in advance. Then you can work by signing with a friend.

The Right Ways To Succeed In Network Marketing

To get success in network marketing we have to take decision. Yes, I have to work in this and if you start doing it with full faith and dedication, then you will get success. In my opinion telling you a great point You see this

1. Use products yourself first.

- Always take your own advice.
- Tell people about the brand and about the business knowledge.
- Always go to the meeting seminar to learn.
- Continue working hard with his team.
- Stay away from these negative thinkers
- Follow-up all your commerce and distributors.
-
-
- Use company's products – The first thing is to use company's products because until you don't know about the products, your faith will not be strong, that's why most of all about the taste of products and its best quality and range First you must have faith in it. As you use yourself, you will get some better results for yourself, then your wealth will increase on your own and will also increase on company's roads and your faith will increase on company's too. And as soon as your trust increases, your confidence will also increase, as your confidence increases, you will be able to make more and more people and your business will grow with a great goodwill, due to which you will achieve success.

- Always take advice from your store- Store in network marketing is called for your right guide in this business. and if your
- Store is with you i.e. even if both of you join on the same day, you should take advice from store only and thank them daily because in this business you will get more success if you learn from store's guide line. If the future does not satisfy you, then you can take yourself and your team forward by learning from your successful upline. Since most of the time the person who will bring you network marketing success is the person. That's why if you always do what the voice says, then your success is certain.
- Tell more and more people about your products and business knowledge to new people- See, the more people you tell about products, the more your waistline will become. The more friends you make, the more you will have deductees.
- It is important to keep in mind that first of all you have to make friends, relatives, neighbors and all the people you know, and then you have to meet them directly. Do not go because you will not be able to satisfy them if you ask anything because you do not have much experience in this. And if you will not be able to satisfy them, they will neither buy products from you nor will they join the business with you. For this, you have to achieve that after making a link, you should take time from your store and stay with them, you should introduce those people to the store and you have to learn with full attention that how your store gives people about products and business knowledge. I tell and how to answer people's questions easily, even after

You can work alone because by the time you make a living doing this you will become the king of this business.

- Meetings and Seminars- See this is the most invaluable key to get success in network marketing. That is, it is the first step to give maximum success. Suppose you have started using ads and you have also started working, but how will you give correct information about your ads and business knowledge to the people. If we don't go to the seminar, then by going to the seminar you get the right information about the tips and tricks. So that you can give correct information to the people and you also become satisfied because you see normal people there in the meeting, whether they are sitting there with a rug or doing business, seeing all these people, your satisfaction increases and you also attract new people. If you show seminars then they become distributors with you in doing business with you. And whoever comes to the meeting, then you get to learn their story and how they work in the market. And one has to learn training from different people. The more you learn, the more you will earn. In order to get success in any film, you should learn the nuances of that thing so that you can be successful. According to my opinion, I used to go to training only to adopt learning formulas which did not give them success so that I do not spend that much time. And those teachers are adopting new formulas by which they are moving forward so that our time is not wasted and success is achieved by following the steps taught by them.
- Keep working hard continuously with your team - This is the best accurate way to get success in network marketing-
- By learning in the training seminars, we together with our

team, by teaching them, by working with them, we should continue to grow our business continuously. Because there is a saying that in your team if you work with your team with hard work and dedication then your team will also work together with their team.

- If everyone continues to work like this together, then it is not known that your level means that you start getting more and more. And working with the team keeps the team spirited. And disappointment does not spread in the whole team and seeing you, many leaders are prepared in your team, due to which money starts coming to your house and your team's house and life starts changing. By doing this, your team gets bigger and you become a successful leader and your name starts appearing and when you and your leaders get respect on promotion, they start getting all the happiness in the world.

- Stay away from negative minded people - In the beginning, this industry was maligned by many people. Many women have brought a bad name to this India. But the real time of this indie is now which is going on now and in present time if you can work in this indie in any way. In today's time business and monsoon like this industry, your promotion is not found anywhere else in other industry and due to this many people are also negative about it, so you have to stay away from such people. And some people joined the girls but did not work with dedication and hard work. Such unsuccessful people spread negativity, one should always stay away from such people.

And you work with all your hard work and dedication and get success

- Follow-up is necessary- You have to follow-up whether you are your waist or your dieter. Because the most beautiful thing in this business is the follow-up because there is no such business or industry where there is follow-up except this industry.

If you follow up on your waist regularly, you will know Getting the best results starts. Due to which you start getting results. That is, from that room other rooms become closer to you. And if you follow-up better, then it is possible that he becomes your distributor and if a distributor is made with a proper ridge, then he becomes your faithful distributor.

9

Mohit Upadhyay - Why to do network marketing?

"Right now, at this very moment, you can make the decisive beginning which will later propel you to the pinnacle of success, that beginning is nothing but the beginning of small changes within yourself"

It can be such changes through which there is a continuous flow of excitement and enthusiasm inside you and you start showing the agility to walk on the less path. You started feeling the need to get love every moment.

your own dreams,—

seek advice from people who are experienced in this. people who are. As you start moving towards making your dreams come true, you will start to feel that very soon you will get rid of all those things which you have been doing compulsively. In which you never feel joy. Get it. Therefore, if you get a chance to fulfill the work you were dreaming of, then you will be elated to bring about a dramatic change in your life. For that it is highly recommended that you like to become already successful.

The torch bearers who have faced the difficulties and challenges that come in that way before you. The company of such people will be very important for you. They know what kind of obstacles come in the way sometimes. Sometimes you have to work with enthusiasm and sometimes with your senses. To give the right direction to your enthusiasm, the company of your guide will be no less than a boon for you.

Is enthusiasm enough?

It is not enough to have passion to achieve success.   Along with this, strength, commitment, determination, unity, plans, personal development and continuous activity are also very important. You must have a strong ambition and a dream in your eyes and must overcome obstacles like self misconceptions and negative surroundings to make it come true.

Perhaps you do not realize how much power there is in choice and commitment. Athletes from all over the world choose to train day and night for four years for the Olympics to be held every four years and then move towards the goal with full dedication and commitment.

you have to choose—-

You have to choose whether you are satisfied with the life you are living or not. If you are not satisfied, it means that you want something else from your life. You want to achieve something even greater. Maybe you want a luxurious house where you want to spend a lot of time with your family members. Maybe you want to get influential by earning more money.

Maybe you want to wish for a very unique tomorrow.

be it love or

to fight or to flee,

fast or slow,

mobility or inertia

success or failure,

life or death,

Lose or win...

Everything starts with choosing only.

So choose whatever you want to paste, write it on a card and keep it with you always or stick it on your bathroom mirror. So that the card constantly reminds you.

Search — for your dreams ——

Network Marketing is the only platform that not only helps you fulfill your dreams but is also determined to make them come true. For that it is necessary to first search for your own dreams.

Do you know someone who has a lot of enthusiasm and a desire to do something new, but does not know how to start?

This is a common problem, most of the people are not able to search for themselves.

You are interested in some things but you know and under-stand and don't see what you want?

How to start this process of knowing and understanding? But it is very easy, first of all do something in which you enjoy, you feel blissful, in the same way you will see the path and on that path you will see the destination clearly.

Try doing one thing, with the help of which you can know that what you want to achieve in life, write on a piece of paper.

On the left side, write down 5 to 10 things you are forced to do—

And on the right side mention what you want to achieve in life i.e. your dreams—

As—-

Circumstances and dreams.

- Boring job - bored with the job.
- Old car - a new car.
- Debt - Economic freedom.

Now draw a big cross on the pen with the condition. And focus all your energy on your dreams which you want to achieve.

You will see amazing results. Challenges are suddenly opening up, Difficulties are going away. Now the day is not far when you will be very close to your destination.

Your imagination is the fuel to your dreams.

Network marketing has been important. The power of your will "If you know clearly what you want to achieve, it is very easy to achieve it. Your power is an effective tool, it can get you out of the basic situation and become the engine of your dreams. Six athletes who win medals in the Olympics anticipate their success from years in advance. A study has shown that the athletes of East Germany and Russia used to spend 75% of their time in anticipation of success. Today, many professional athletes spend more and more time daydreaming about winning. This is how they mentally prepare themselves for victory.

The mental image of success -

Leave your hands and feet loose for a while and relax, relax, draw an arrow of success, a mental image of your success in your mind, see yourself enjoying all the things you aspire for. Feel like you are driving that expensive car which is your dream to sit in. All those beautiful places in the world, where it is your dream to visit. Let it be that you are roaming there with complete economic freedom, let it be that you are being called on the stage with thunderous applause in every function, let it be that your energy and ability have developed so much that now you Giving importance in seminars, showing people the path of success. Deeply feel those moments of joy and imagine what that experience would be like.

What kills dreams ?

Misconceptions

You don't understand that challenges provide us an opportunity to learn and grow. You make misconceptions that stifle your dreams. Misconceptions kill you. And you must have seen that some people make their dreams come true while some people are not able to. Perhaps they are unable to because some misconceptions prevent them from moving forward and taking risks. It creates such a mountain of dreams inside that all the dreams die amidst them.

Wrong beliefs, the answer is not that simple, it is some childhood experiences that narrow your thinking. Many a times parents unknowingly give wrong information to us." If you don't pass these numbers then you will be of no use" or "Advertisement for job is going on without it you will not get job" The parents are not intentionally planting the seeds of misconceptions in your mind, they are doing what they think is right, they want to encourage and accept everything they say as truth.

Generally you do not find such guides who explain to you about the challenges of life that without facing the challenges, neither you can learn anything nor can you grow. That is why misconceptions start growing in your mind, which withers your dreams as well as your dreams. Instead of moving ahead considering it as the ladder of success, you start thinking and considering every obstacle as the reason for your failure. that you can never win.

Mostly you start following many beliefs in your youth like "I am good" I will not get what I want, or no one wants me. It does not have any positive benefit. Such misconceptions some-times go deep inside your subconscious mind and it becomes extremely dangerous. In such a situation, you destroy your possibilities and become indifferent towards your dreams and start making excuses.

So you have to find out which misconceptions exist inside you and you have to find out and replace them with positive thoughts. As you identify the misconceptions inside, you will come to know that what a huge bundle of lies is present inside you. Give it your time. And don't forget to laugh at your misconceptions. This will loosen his negative grip on you.

Talk to your guide.

Think deeply about yourself.

Denial can lead to your misconceptions_

- Only rich people can make their dreams come true.
- Only educated or college holders can make their dreams come true
- Only people with recommendations and contacts can make their dreams come true
- Only learners succeed.
- Only people can succeed.
- Only those who have a lot of time can make their dreams come true.
- Those who have a lot of residence only can get success.
- Those who are well organized. Only they can be successful.
- Only extremely talented people can be successful.
- Only networking people are successful.
- Only people who take risks can succeed.
- Only for those who look beautiful, their dreams get true
- Successful people are unable to give time to family.
- Only people with passion are successful.

Similar misconceptions creep into your mind. You might be laughing at them.

But it is true that such misconceptions do not show any way to your subconscious mind. Know them, challenge them and make your dreams come true through network marketing.

You must laugh

Someone has said that laughter is a must, laughter is the most effective medicine. Therefore, by laughing at misconceptions, you can reduce their impact to a great extent. Think about the concepts written above and see how many common concepts are wrong with them.

Some of these beliefs make no sense at all, they are completely wrong, then you are a fool to take your misconceptions so seriously.

Laugh at them, think of them as a joke, and you will see that slowly- Slowly all this is disappearing from your subconscious mind.

Have the courage to do what is impossible for you— Dream , Vision, Mission, and The objective.

Sometimes you think that how can I talk about my dreams or how can I share them with people, then for this the discussion is going on. That first you understand the mission and vision of your life. Your vision, mission, and mission are all tied to your values, the values that mean the most to you.

Your vision is the reflection of what you want from life. It is the mental arrow of your hopes and dreams. God has said that those who do not have reason cannot live. Their life is nothing but a voice inside you that tells you again and again that you have to do this or be this in life. .

And when you want to fulfill your life purpose with full dedication and enthusiasm. Then it becomes your mission.

Thinking is what your vision can be? Your vision may be about the future of your business i.e. network marketing that will be the future of your business in the coming days? You have to think that in the coming days I would have a different identity in my network marketing.

There is some reason behind every goal, that reason can be and still be, if you remain famous in the fulfillment of your goal, then you will not only use your ability and energy but will also improve the lives of others along with yourself. Will also feel deeply.

do work to get ahead

David Henry says, "Incidents and circumstances are the cause of their rise, we ourselves, they rise from the seeds we sow."

After choosing network marketing, like it, do not look at yourself with inferiority complex. Because people will say that this is the job you were given to do, don't bother yourself with it.

You will see and feel that there is a deep connection between them and your favorite activities in your life. And it's even compatible. We get satisfaction from doing mindful work. And our ego increases. It becomes somewhat easier to fulfill them in our lives.

Many people remain unhappy with their work because none of their dreams are being fulfilled in that work. That means there is no match between life and its values. If this is the case with you too, then there is nothing to panic. You have to take steps and walk in such a situation immediately. Where in future you will be working according to your mind. Such actions that your life will be matching them. Then it will not be a difficult task for you to fulfill them in life.

Till date no dream has ever come true without doing less. So you have to do less. You have to move forward, you have to be dynamic continuously, no dream can ever be fulfilled by sitting at one place.

And it is in such moments that the process of creative thinking begins within us. As you move towards fulfillment. By the way, you have to go on capturing those creative ideas in your mind. and be responsible for making all your dreams come true

Negative thinking

Negative thinking is a sad state that many of us fall prey to, we think negatively because that's what we've been taught, we've grown up in a culture that's based on punishments rather than rituals, plus we're told there is something lacking in our life. If we look around us, we see various kinds of people and things which we continuously keep giving both positive and negative suggestions. Now we humans have a habit that in which We wish to do the work that is prohibited, that is why we ourselves allow negative thoughts to come inside us.

Our mind is divided into two parts, one part is called positive i.e. positive and the other part is called negative.

So you have to tame them. If you succeed in taming them, they become your slaves. And fulfills your every wish, burns you with new energy and success in life, creates a glow of confidence on your face, tells you that your whole world is very beautiful.

Now let's talk about negatives. Negatives are of soft nature, you don't need to work hard to use them, they accept your words immediately. But their special thing is that you cannot make them your slave, they themselves make you their slave, then they become whatever they want, they make you lazy, hesitant, angry, irritable and tell you that the world is full of darkness, you are poor, your health is bad, you have done what God made you like this, and don't know what is giving negative messages to your mind.

How to stop negative thoughts from entering you

This is a great question, whose answer everyone wants to know. First of all know that we are the master of our mind, our mind is like a house. In which whatever thought comes, first takes permission from us, without our permission, no thought can come to mind in any way, if we want, no negative thought can come to our mind. The best way to stop a thought from entering us is to not allow it to enter us at all.

Suppose someone holding a ball of fire in his hand asks you to take this ball of fire in your hand. So you touch it in your hand. I know you will never do that, because? As such

Doing this will burn your hand. Let's think for once that you have given permission to take the ball of fire in your hand. So it will happen for 2 seconds, then the hand will not get burnt. Only the temperature of your hand will increase. But after 2 seconds the hand will start burning. If you still do not leave that ball of fire from your hand then the temperature will increase by itself and gradually it will spread in your whole body then you will not know anything can not do. Similarly, people from outside keep putting negative thoughts in our mind. Now it is up to you to think that by holding those negative thoughts, you want to set your life on fire with those thoughts, because of those thoughts. Or else by not allowing these negative thoughts to enter your mind, you want to make your life as cool and bright as a moon with positive thoughts.

Effective positive affirmations -

Using a dull positive wrap is not going to do any good, it is more likely to cause harm, for example look at the idea "I'm trying to buy a new car with the least amount of money" "This wrap is very loose and Faded. You can also say this in this way "I am trying to buy a great new car at a low price". You are telling your point of view that you should get his arrow is very clear in your mind, for this it is positive or effective.

Always keep positive statements in the present tense. you your present If you improve then only your future will improve. You have to live in the present. Future lies in the present, not in the past. If you do something, you will get its fruits in the future.

You will remain empty handed. That's why it is continuing. Your affirmative sentences should be in present tense. For example, use "I was today" and not "I will be tomorrow".

Make an image of your success,-

Now is the time to take a decisive step in the direction of your fulfillment and use the very effective tool you have now called "Dream Collage" to achieve success.

Some people also call dream collage as a bubble or map because it is a concrete representation of dreams coming true. This is a great way to motivate yourself. For this take a board or foam sheet on which But if you want, put your favorite colored paper, then put such pictures and words on it that show the fulfillment of your dreams.

Make your dream collage to make your dream come true, here are some suggestions, first of all put your and your life partner's arrow in the middle of the pole.

Then below your arrow put the title of the position you want to achieve through your network marketing.

Place 'cutouts' of your dream home, jewellery, vehicles or anything .Write down some more favorite states, such as 'healthy and happy' ' 'debt issues' or 'financially stressed' or 'family time' or 'freedom to travel to favorite places'.

When your dream collage is completed, draw an arrow of it, then put some of its pictures in the house and keep some in your wallet. Seeing the real form of your dreams again and again will give you inspiration and take your mind. Will keep on towards.

Remember-

There is a fire inside you, when this fire is kindled, then its spark blazes within you, this burning passion becomes the fuel of your life, you or your mission, then you can reach the heights of the sky within your reach. You aspire to achieve the greatest success, and with the help of your boom and bust, you move forward crossing the obstacles on the way. But your aim remains firm. And you know that There is no goal in the world that you cannot achieve.

others, because you have the seeds of greatness within you, and when that You will make a positive difference in your life as well as in the lives of seed is about to unfold, nothing can stop you. You will be on the cusp of success, because you have The enthusiasm is blazing! That passion can change your life! The whole world can change!!

Friends, with the help of this book 'Network Marketing Ek Viral Yug', you can make yourself the uncrowned king of network marketing. Here all our friends have played the field of network marketing and have gained sweet experiences from so many years. After working on it, I have shared it with all of you. If you

are not very educated, you do not have much money, you do not have much connection, then there is no need to worry even if you have power, here you will get everything. Money, social prestige, social security, economic freedom to roam.

For financial freedom and your dreams come true, then friends, what are you waiting for, choose Network cum Marketing Sector and make your unfulfilled dreams come true.

10

Shekhar Jain - Do you want to be successful in direct selling?

R obert Kiyosaki tells in his book Rich Dad Poor Dad that there are 4 ways to earn money and if there is any best way in those ways then it is direct which is also called passive income. This is the method where after working hard for a period of time, money starts coming continuously throughout life. This is its special thing which attracts most of the people towards itself. In this technique the team works which benefits the whole team.

Today crores of people in India and abroad are associated with direct and earn lakhs of crores of rupees from direct.

Do you also want to be successful in this technique?

Sure I can understand that you also want to be successful. Those who want to be successful in direct selling again, now I am going to tell the truth.

Listen carefully.

I am going to tell you 5 tasks. If you are told 5 things

If you can do it with full dedication, with your will, then surely you can be successful in the direct business. Task

1 - Keep working:

If you have joined any direct then in any case keep working because people are watching you. Whether money comes or not, keep working because people are watching you. Whether people listen to you or not, keep working because people are watching you. Whether people join you or not, keep working because people are watching you. Whether your leaders support you or not, keep working because people are watching you. And when people are watching you, they see your success and failure. Let's see your work, see your residence. And when you are awake from the inside, then people may not connect with you in the beginning, but when they see you working, then they also slowly keep connecting with you. That's why keep doing what.

Task 2 - Keep Learning:

What you are today is because of your knowledge and if you live somewhere in some other world tomorrow, that too will definitely be because of your knowledge. That's why if the knowledge increases in life, then definitely the place will also increase. In order for direct selling programs to be successful, we continue to learn. Keep learning to keep yourself motivated. Keep learning to accept people's "no". Keep learning to maintain composure in every situation.

When a person working as a peon in a bank can while learning by become the manager of the same bank, then you can also become learning the uncrowned king of direct while learning.

When a 16 year old boy can become Sachin Tendulkar while learning, when a waiter can become a superstar Akshayy Kumar while learning, you too can become a direct superstar while learning, so keep learning and today In this digital age it is very easy to learn anything new. If anything is needed to learn something new, then only one thing and that is willpower.

If you go to YouTube alone, the knowledge of well-known motivational speakers from India and abroad is available free of cost. You can be successful by watching those videos.

Do 3 - Keep the conversation going:

And it has been observed that the distance between the stars increases due to one reason and that reason is non-interaction with each other. Research tells that if you remain in constant contact with your people, then the kind of problem you want to be solved, the solution is found. So stay in touch in any case.

In direct it is seen that the leader thinks that my down line should talk to me and the one who is in the down line thinks that my leader should call me and talk to me.

Because of this small thinking, we keep distance from our own people knowingly and unknowingly, which ultimately harms us in future. That's why stay connected with your people on one pretext or the other. He kept doing one thing or the other and kept talking to people.

It is not necessary in conversation that all the time we should only talk about our network or business. The conversation can be related to any topic related to family, social or country and abroad. If you ask me that any 10 names

Tell me immediately and I will suggest the names of those people with whom you are in close contact.

That's why your name will be on top of the list of people whom you keep remembering or with whom you keep talking. Certainly the people with whom you are in constant contact will always come forward to cooperate with you.

Work 4 - Behave yourself:

Whether it is about life or direct sale. In the end, people only remember your behavior.

When a person leaves this world, people talk about that person only one of the two. Either everyone says about this man that what a great man he was or else people will say

The person who died was not A maniac.

Friends, I want to tell one thing that people value your behavior more than your money, education and knowledge. That's why it is important that we maintain our behavior. In any case, maintain your best behavior with us.

Let us not spoil our path even by mistake from anyone. If you cannot do good to someone, then at least do not speak bad words. The easiest formula to maintain good behavior with everyone is to always treat people the way you expect people to treat you.

Under direct, we do not even know that which person will be useful in our life. If you want more and more people to be associated with you in your happiness and sorrow, then it is necessary that all of us Maintain better behavior with him.

Will always be with you as long as our behavior is correct towards them. People who have joined you, are right connected or are about to join. all those people

Action 5 - Keep correcting your mistake:

It has been said that to err is human nature. There will be no such person in this world who has never committed any mistake in his life. Every person must have made at least one mistake at some point in his life. That's why it is never a wrong thing to make a mistake but it is definitely a wrong thing to repeat your mistake.

Make mistakes, recognize the mistake and keep correcting your mistakes. This has to be done if you want to move forward in life. That is why it has also been said that if the forgotten in the morning returns home in the evening, then it is not called forgotten.

At some point in life, if you feel that you have reduced your work, then it does not matter, increase your speed again. If you ever feel that you have stopped learning, then start learning again. This thing is easy.

11

Jasveer Kumar - Changing business of a changing era

C hanging business of a changing era. In today's 20th century, with the changing era, businesses have also started changing! Where earlier people were engaged in their work with hard work of the body, today a big change has been seen in them too! Today the same work is being done by all the machines!

In this age of computers and mobiles, another big revolution has been brought between hard work and smart work.

Perhaps the hard work is more than before, but of the mind! hours work in minutes

Meanwhile, another big revolution came in direct.

direct selling

In 2017, going through bad times, I too fell in love with the world of direct!

The incident happened in such a way that I did not even know that this was happening, I was just watching. Work from home for 2 hours and earn 10000 -15000 per month

Crores of millions of people come and listen and tell people and there they laugh By becoming in the company of useless people, they would have become like that!

But due to going to the training, I had understood one thing that work is not bad, it is necessary to understand, not to relax the passion of learning! this is where the topic begins

****

You have to learn

In this changing era of 21st century, the way of working has changed, earlier the work which was done manually in many months by hard work, the same work is being done by machines in hours, minutes and seconds in today's era of science.

Talking about the income of those who get the work done by the machines and those who run the machines, we get to hear that *dal roti* is being made! Now let's talk about those who have these machines, their condition is somewhat better than these because a network works under them of 2 or more people who are on salary.

Here we now talk about a business which has left all these behind.

****

direct selling

As soon as the era of this indie came, a big revolution came, it proved that to be rich, one should not be educated, this indie made 1% people believe that a person can really do anything. This proved no less than a magic, let's know about this magic

Both, this is such an industry in which if a person works hard continuously for 2-3 years, then it has proved to be a hen that lays golden eggs every day!

In the language of common people, it is also called the work of connecting members! It is also called the work of trapping some negative people by telling lies or lies! Because they do not even know that there is a network! It has power! If you try to explain, then he thinks that this is nonsense!

Now let's talk about him, if he is a farmer, he sowed paddy seed today itself, if he is asked to grind it into flour today itself, then he may feel guilty! He may even laugh! Maybe he will fall on our throats!

If he is a sensible farmer, he will explain that it has just been sown! Now it needs a lot of hard work and time till it ripens, then it will be sold in the market, then it will reach you, then do whatever you want.

This is all we have to learn, we have to build a successful and intelligent network, we have to understand like a farmer, we have to learn by being intelligent.

Understanding the importance of time, explaining the power of the network, we have to build a network one by one and repeat the same work every year, there is a network working behind every big person.

Like the Prime Minister himself.

Now see for yourself, do they do all the work alone, don't they have a team of their own?

The bigger his income. So here is this! Now the matter talking about the real world, let's take a successful farmer, how many laborers work, that is his network, the professional who works with a shopkeeper, that is his network, and there are millions of examples, the bigger the network,

direct selling

Before coming into the world of direct, you need a good and legal way to identify it, the fault of the load! company's Profile! Owner's!

You get knowledge of all these things through seminars.

You get the information from the person who told you about it

Now the thing is, you have to learn it for some time, you have to do as you are told, then slowly one by one you also have to do the same thing that people above you have been doing, people will come and go, buy something, refuse something By doing this work for two to three years, you become a network, it depends on your way of working, your attitude, your hard work, on you! Your power and your image reflects your identity

You become a successful networker.

Now there is a lot more to learn in this, which is taught to you by different leaders in different seminars according to your level.

Level is important in this, the higher the level, the higher his income, hence it is also called MLM .

Here you are given some targets to increase your level, by completing which you can raise your level, you can take foreign tour or you get the reward or bonus whatever you have placed on achieving the level. To achieve that, you have to develop the qualities of a successful networker.

What are those
qualities?

1. Your body language
2. Your projection
3. Language
4. Your Lifestyle
5. Your dress-up

Such qualities that you have to learn, due to which your image becomes even more bright, it is work on yourself, now
let's talk about the team, you are also responsible for them.

- Timely follow up
- Focus
- Timing
- Monitoring

like the work you have to do on the team
Importance of part time and full time
If you do it full time with very little hard work
yes you can succeed
If you do it part time means you can achieve success in 2-3 years by taking out 2 hours of time along with your profession. Passionate people do this too.
who can do this job?
This can be done by every person who wants to do something in his life, who has some dreams, who has some fire.
He is hardworking, he has the desire to change himself, every man can do this work.
And yes, remember this thing that this is not a game of balls, in this game also many people have created history, you get all this power from their biography.
Like- Sandeep Maheshwari, Vivek Binndra, Sonu Sharma etc. is an example.

positivity and negativity

Everyone can do this work, but the one who will be successful, is the one who will be active, who will have passion, who will have fire in his dreams, who does not understand anything by negative people, who will follow the calculation.

Unsuccessful people are those who are negative, after some time they go back to their environment from which they have to get out.

Ratio

The ratio works in this article, this ratio is different for each person, it works according to their system, as told to 100 people.

50 heard

40 noticed

30 people came to the system

20 people engaged

10 successful

Now seeing the success of 10, 100 people came again, this way it goes on.

and it has to go on and on

Success is not found in doing any work but by doing it again and again.

In this work, some tools have to be made to promote your business.

The person who pays attention to this moves closer to success

To be successful you have to deserve success

To become successful, it is also necessary to stay in the company of successful people, read their biography, focus on your habits, while doing this work, you become addicted to it.

If this behavior of yours continues correctly, then success comes inwards.

Challenges

Challenges will inevitably come in any great work

One has to take care to face them, a person learns from every mistake.

If mistakes keep repeating then you will not succeed

People will also laugh at you, even you will be disappointed, but don't let the worm inside you die, he should keep saying only one thing.

History is full of great people, there is a need to study, there is a need to learn

what will people say

People will say the world's biggest disease

Before doing any work, we think that what will people say, the neighborhood will laugh.

Now you need to think here for whom you are working

For those who are or for yourself

Even before this they were the same, it doesn't matter if it takes two more years to laugh, but you should have the power to stop their laughter.

These people are those people whose work is that they should not do anything, they should not be above us.

the decision is in your hands what to do

Life is yours

If you have a life, then why do you bother about people, get up and change the history in your generation, so that in time to come, your grandchildren can proudly say that our grandparents were a networker, people can be seen giving examples by telling the reasons of your success.

Once a person from the foreign started trading in Key rings.

While starting he booked a big deal in which his bracelets fell short, he asked another money merchant that I need bracelets worth one lakh, you tell me, will you deal with us?

The merchant said yes and the deal was finalized and the bracelets were counted, packed and sent by sea.

Said brother, tell me the matter

Said that the bangle that was sent, its packing is open, I was supposed to make a profit of four paise, so many bangles must have gone away in it.

The merchant laughed and said, I would have counted first, there is still a chance, count is complete.

how can you say that with such confidence

Said brother, I will tell you later, first count

the rings were complete

Contacted again and said, tell me where did these codes come from

Said this is the string of our fists, one flies, the other pulls his leg

the third flies the fourth pulls his leg

We don't even allow humans to fly, they are strict

So you have to avoid these leg pullers

Success will come

keep faith patience interest courage hard work passion positive thinking continues

keep trusting in god

You will go from zero to hero in the world of direct selling.

Why is it called direct selling ?

If you describe in detail, then I will tell you on the basis of an example, suppose there is a shopkeeper in your city or village, let us take an example from him; how much does it cost in company

Yes, it will be worth it in a little

By adding his profit of Rs.2, company sold it in the market for Rs.5, now he is a wholesaler. Through agents, he sold to the shopkeeper for certain Rs. Just understand this.

Direct selling does not do all this, direct selling means buying any item from direct means, which means people who are grabbing money in the middle will now be left in your pocket, you have to teach people to save this, because of this, this directly gets customers.

you get the team

And the motion of the brand keeps on happening, this is direct selling.

Some people take it too seriously no brother don't want to do this, rather let's do this business

It has changed the lives of millions of people

That's why it is called a life-changing business, on which even some negative people laugh.

laugh laugh

But remember this world, which has laughed at, has also created history as a witness.

We are proud that we also belong to that India today.

Events

While doing this work, some such incidents also happen due to which negativity will try to come to you, but staying here is also successful.

Like..... many times the family members also say that people should leave this work.

If people join then they run away

You do so much work that you do not get money

People will provoke your family members

But remember one thing, only those people do this work, who have no work

what you do at work they don't have time to talk so much

People wearing coats

Many people also call the people of this city by the name of the suitmen.

Now if seen, this is a sign or identity of how a businessman would dress.

Doctors, lawyers, policemen, all these would have been recognized by care, then coat, tie, belt, shoes, fitting, fitness is the dress and identity of a business man, but some negative creatures have said that they are used to rob people. wear coats and pants

Here also you will get negative energy but remember

You have to keep doing your work.

This direct selling is selling both are like an ocean its ideology which has no end.

To play this game, either a player is required or he has to become a player, if both cannot be done, forget that you can do something big.

Playing this game is like winning the battle of Mahabharata.

If you want to pass, you have to learn.

companies ask for money

Hahahahaha..... I can't stop laughing when this topic comes up

And it has been seen that the ideology of the people of this country is that they ask for money.

First of all let me say that this is the misconception of the people

Suppose a networker talks to someone about part time work, there if the person in front puts this question that how to do this work, then he will have to talk about Investment, if not then he will say that at least not before.

If told then.... Illusion has been born, understand —- which one?

That they ask for money

Now I will also give some medicine to their illusions.

First of all, we don't go to anyone by walking means

Don't take the initiative, when the person in front asks you something, you have to tell.

As far as money is concerned, let me tell you that this money is not for us but for you only.

Let's talk about business outside the world of direct selling, believe that if those people want to set up a traditional business, according to today's era

If a grocery shopkeeper has to do at least 2-3 lakh rupees, then he will have to do it.

So what is the guarantee that it will work

So what is the guarantee that you will earn lakhs in a single day

Now, if we were to talk about direct selling, it would be very small here

Without money, you can't even get a needle, and how can you get crores, and the matter of success, if you follow the system and do this work with hard work, even by mistake, then here I would have stood first in the queue of those who would have taken the guarantee that you will get success

Just think, understand, apply your mind, don't be a leg puller

Sir, if you want to jump in a well, its depth cannot be measured, if you jump in a well, you will fall.

People don't listen these words.

And such questions are also heard.

If people don't listen to me, then you tell me, you tell those who want to listen.

who are those people where to find them

no where sir these are those people

It's just that you have to be able to tell

If your image is the same where you are living, then there is no need to go anywhere.

If the image is bad, then go away from that place and go to a different place where people are unknown.

You have done this work with honesty and pride and returned after creating a good life by making an image among the people, then look, even those who do not like you will learn by joining you.

If you are not getting success then don't change the job, change the way of working

Change your eyes and your views will change

The edges will change for god's sake.

Weeping

Remember, God has given the same time to those too, whose names are spoken in history.

God has given the same amount of time to those, seeing whom you think how much time is there.

God has given them the same amount of time as you

what world do you live in that you don't have time

even if there is no time.

Do you think in vain that when will our day come?

Life is yours, sir, you will also have to spend your time .

I have time but I don't have money .

Sir, if there is no money to live life, how have you lived till date?

If you don't agree, then you have to do direct only to earn money.

family members will not agree

What is it that you will have to persuade, you don't have to persuade sir, you have to understand, but before that you have to become sensible.

Hey brother, if nothing would have been done, then today these people who protest despite all odds, they are fools, they are also doing the same, you also have to do the same.

And what you have done earlier, now don't do that, earlier you used to do it for your own pleasure, now it will be done for your sake.

Such excuses are seen and heard.

Their crying is also justified, the reason for this is also that they will bring in the world of direct selling, who themselves not only give a bad name to the end, because they themselves start doing it without learning.

Now it is your matter, if you curse God, God, you have not given me anything, then remember that God's answer will be the same as for how many people you had taken the offer of dear selling, but you were the one who didn't even listen to my negative.

My name is Jasveer Sharma, Belonging to Tupura Sahib, a small historical village in Moge district of Punjab, I grew up in a middle class family from Rajasthan, my father used to do the duty of a reader in Gurudwara Sahib, but my economic condition was good.

Because the one whose parents are with him, no one can be richer in this world, it was not a matter of money, sir, in the world where he lived, everyone was the same, so he never got angry with God for anything.

Yes, my dreams were very big from my childhood, I got fond of writing songs, I did not know how that sad song came, I thought that if someone sings my songs, then my name will be there.

Means one thing became clear that I wanted a name in my life.

But I did not know how to search for a platform

I didn't even have enough money to find myself

just kept writing

While doing this, the phase of life passed by, when I grew up, I did not even know what to study, I was class 10th, but even there there was no focus that how much to study and what to become.

Only one thing kept troubling me, I want to become big

but how else

did not know this

This is the beginning of the journey of success, the day you came to know what your reasons are, no one can stop you from moving forward.

I got my questions answered

It was that there should be a lot of money, time, luxury and comfort.

people know me for good deeds

After completing my 10th standard, my mind was so set that I started working in a shop where I was so inclined towards marketing that I didn't even feel like studying.

Just seeing the money started thinking of increasing this money.

In the same way I went to a big city where my salary was coming. 3 years have passed, but this problem is not complete, but I kept getting money from work, but it also kept coming and going, then I thought that I have come from doing job, or should I do my own work, then more money will come.

I removed myself from there after 3 years and after coming to my city my father got me started my business and by God's grace I am very happy.

Come

3 years later he called it my mistake or ignorance that it was a great job

Just another year I went to do business but I could not succeed in it.

writing was still in business for the second time

didn't let the worm inside die

Then got a job and job of job and business of business

It was also there and earned money, made up for the losses incurred in the business.

After 3 years, she also lost her lineage due to some reason.

The economic condition started deteriorating;

I didn't even know what to do

I got married, I got a child, that too was passing, I failed for the third time in my life.

But the worm was still fluttering that you can do something that will make everything alright

That was a favor from my father

who always supported me

Due to him, I once again decided to do the work of which I wanted to become a lyricist since childhood.

Home small, then moved to a metro city, among strangers through social media, those people turned out to be very good;

The journey began and I joined as a songwriter among some people

In this journey of life, big and small things happened which squeezed me completely from inside.

Now the name has started to be made but the money was still waiting

2.5 years have passed then suddenly another turning point came where I was supposed to gain wealth and fame but at the same time time played its turn, in the next 6 months my rent was ruined i.e. again 3 years

I got broken, life became a joke, it became a spectacle among people, poverty came so much that I started working as a

laborer for 3 years, then suddenly another turning point came, where again a ray of hope arose.

then encouraged and consulted father

Father again patted me on the back.

It was a different world its view was different there everything was what I wanted the biggest thing was what was there

Name

wealth

fame

independence

and a glimpse of another life

Now think how much power will be in MLM

I did it with a lot of hard work and condition, but sir, when God gives it, then there should be interest in handling it, if this person does not have it, then he will come and go.

sir will go

Everything given in 3 years direct selling was achieved, just delay was to put hash tag

Again the same thing repeated my mistakes and now it has failed here too

So direct is bad

so it was a hoax

So was it just a lie, no

sir, there was a flaw in the character.

Needed to recognize my mistakes

Sitting alone in the car, I understood in such a way that where is the mistake?

Then started working on them till now

the whole world had understood that it

is as easy as it is to get this thing, it is just a matter of time to learn.

That's all, learned, understood and understood the network, its power and

Then started direct in a

different way but didn't stop working, sir didn't stop

learning and till now I am moving towards success where there is no hindrance, think before doing every work

I keep learning and then everything is given by God, then why

is it that when a person like me can succeed in the world of selling, then you are intelligent and intelligent.

just hundred

It has to be learned,

it has to be networked

there will be mistakes

also have to improve

it will take time

But remember, if there is fire inside you, there

is a worm, then do not let it die, the day that worm dies, sir, you will die while alive.

I wished that it should flourish and flourish. May God keep everyone happy.

When Hanuman ji did not know about the Sanjivani herb, he

had brought the mountain and brought it at the feet of the Lord.

If again the network gets messed up then try one more thing which Hanuman ji has

done. By doing this, I think you can also earn lakhs of rupees per month.

if still not sure

So here's the only solution I have thought

12

Akshay Bhabutkar - What is Digital Marketing? And how can we define it?

First of all we will see what is digital marketing. Digital marketing means digital marketing of any type of service means doing it online. Today's companies mostly pay for digital marketing. In today's time everything has gone online. Internet has made our life better. Now-a-days, if we want to go somewhere, we book tickets online sitting at home in just 2 minutes. Nowadays, we are able to do any work online in a very easy way, such as online shopping, recharge, bill payment, etc. We can do many things through internet. If you look at the market, more than 90% of the shops research their products online before buying or taking any service and then decide whether to buy or not. If you want to buy something, First of all you search online, see the reviews of that brand, watch videos and then decide whether to buy the brand or not. In such a situation, digital marketing becomes very important for any company or any business. We do digital marketing through the internet.

We can connect with mobile, laptop, tablet, website advertisements or any other application. With digital marketing, we can reach our products or services to a large number of people in a very short time, this is the special thing about digital marketing. We can also call it online marketing. What the customers are looking for, where is the interaction of the customers, what age group people like and what they do not like, we can do all this with digital marketing. In today's time digital marketing has become inward. Every internet has come online. Right now there is no time to meet people, but nowadays the same people meet on social media, talk online because nowadays everyone has become digital.

Everyone is connected to the internet and they are using the internet easily. Looking at these things, the demand for digital marketing is increasing very fast. It takes a lot of time for the customers to go to the market and buy the same product, they can buy the same product online in less time sitting at home, this is also one of the reasons why digital marketing is increasing rapidly. Ask yourself that for how long can you keep yourself away from your mobile and laptop? Time you cannot stay away from your mobile. Most of the important work is done on mobile or laptop only. Now-a-days, people prefer to read the quiz paper more than reading it on mobile or watching videos on YOU TUBE, watching the quiz. If suppose you want to buy a new mobile, first of all you research it online, read about it, watch videos about it and if you like everything, then only you buy the mobile. With digital marketing, we can reach all those things to the people online so that people buy our product.

On the Internet, we can do digital marketing through different websites, sources.

There are some advantages of digital marketing that I would like to tell you,

- 1) True Engine Optimization SEO: Through this we can bring our website or blog on the front page of Google. And if our website comes on the first page, then more people will see the website and buy our product or our service.

- 2) Social Media: Social media is very important such as Facebook, Twitter LinkedIn. Through social media, we can convey our thoughts to the people. We can promote our products on social media so that more and more people come to know about our products and they buy our products. We can reach a large number of people by placing an advertisement of our brand on social media.

- 3) Email Marketing: Giving information about a product or service through email, we can call it email marketing. And by email marketing we can also inform our customers about our upcoming new lines. This email marketing plays a very important role in digital marketing.

- 4) You Tube: You tube is a very popular social media, due to which we can make videos of our brand and reach it to a large number of people. People can also give their opinion by watching the video, we can know how they liked the load or whether it was bad, then we can improve our load accordingly.

- 5) Affiliate Marketing: This is the best way to sell your products in a big way. In this, we can create an affiliate link of our product and place it on a blog or website so that people can buy it. If someone bought that product from our link then we get some % profit.

- 6) Apps marketing: On the Internet, we can make our application accessible to more people. This marketing is very good. People can easily get information about your brand by downloading your app from Google Store. Now a lot of people have photographs. Many big companies make their advertisements and reach people.

- 7) Content Marketing: Motion of content assets which can be used for brand awareness, traffic growth, lead generation in the right way.
- 8) Marketing Automation: Marketing automation is that in which marketing motion is done by using a tool. In which some things like email, social media and other websites and promotions are automated.
- 9) Online PR: Online PR is a method that is used to secure online coverage. Pro, digital promotion, from website These are similar to traditional PR but just in online press.
- 10) Google Ad Words: You must have seen a lot of advertisements on your internet, do you know that most of these advertisements are shown by google. With the help of google ad words, you can do marketing of your product now. This is a paid service, using this you can do marketing of your road very well.
- You can run many types of advertisements through Google adwords. As
- Display advertising
- Text ads
- Image ads
- Text and image ads
- Match content ads
- Video ads
- Pop-up ads
- Sponsored search etc
- Pay Per Click (PPC):

This is such a method, traffic is driven towards your website and promotion, in which you have to pay money if you have ads.

Why is digital marketing important ?

1. This is a simple and fast way to promote your product.
2. Compared to offline marketing, online marketing is different. \
3. You get a lot of income from digital marketing.
4. This is the best way to reach your services to the target audience.
5. In digital marketing, you get thousands of ways to promote your service and product.
6. Digital marketing increases the branding value of your company.
7. This is such a way that sitting at home, you can promote your product globally.
8. With digital marketing, you can sell the product online along with marketing it. And can earn money in many more months.

Digital can be done for all business. Digital marketing works in any industry. Your company is selling something, with the help of digital marketing, you can understand the incoming customers, you can do the work of reaching your product very easily to them.

- 1) For B2B: B2B stands for Business to Business. The main work in this business is online lead generation, in which you have to talk with a salesperson. Here you can bring more and more leads with digital marketing for your business. here you use digital marketing through websites, promotion can bring more and more leads and in very less time.

- 2) For B2C: B2C means Business to Customers. So here the pay man will work that more and more people come to the website and without making their waist through any salesperson.

In this, by creating your website, you can bring more and more people to your website by sitting at home through digital marketing. You can do paid motion with google adwords to bring to the website very easily of any type. And for B2C business social media such as Facebook, Instagram, Twitter and such platforms are very important. By using all these technologies, you can easily reach your customers on your website.

You can get accurate data from digital marketing as compared to any other offline marketing method. If you did offline advertisement or then made a banner and printed it and distributed it among the people. But you will not know that how many people have seen your ad, people from which city have seen your ad, people of which age group have seen your ad, you will not know all this data. But if you run online ad through digital marketing, then you will get a lot of data of your cusotmer like where your ad was shown, in which city it was shown, till you even get your customer's email id and phone number. You can do this, you get a lot more information from digital marketing. That is why today people are earning lakhs of rupees by adopting digital marketing.

You can spread awareness about your brand or about the company to the people.

Like Blog Posts, it is very important to increase your organic traffic. If you do strong SEO and pay proper attention to keywords, then it can give you a lot of benefits. Then we can also spread awareness through infographics to the people. These are also shareable. People keep sharing infographics a lot on social media. After that comes the short video. Many people share these short videos. People share VDO's on WhatsApp. You can mote your videos like this on YouTube.

job in digital marketing

The best thing about digital marketing is that it is an ever growing and never ending business.

Today, digital marketing skills are of great importance in the biggest companies. They are important members of the digital marketing team. And now there is a demand for digital marketing in every company. There are many jobs in digital marketing. If you want to make a virtual marketer, then you have to pay more and more practical work. Digital marketing is a practical fee. You can do job by doing digital marketing but you can also do your own business.